WHAT THEY SA‾
THE BOOKS OF ISA

CW00969215

Quiet Places with Jesus:
40 Guided Imagery Meditations for Personal Prayer

"This book by a former advertising man and lumberjack who became a Roman Catholic priest consists of 40 guided meditations
to help people with personal prayer. Powers's book is a good re-
source for leaders of small groups that meet regularly for prayer
and spiritual growth within and outside the institutional church.
This book is as suitable for non-Catholics as it is for those of the
author's faith."

Frances Stebbins
Roanoke Times & World News

Quiet Places with Mary:
37 Guided Imagery Meditations

"Isaias Powers has done it again! He has skillfully woven together
a collection of elements that results in a truly inspiring prayer
book—a book *of prayer,* a book *for prayer.* Powers demonstrates in
this work an amazing ability to introduce us to the mystery of the
Incarnation in a manner that reverences the divinity and enhances
the humanity of Jesus Christ, through the eyes of his mother,
Mary. This is a book for those who wish to grow in prayer and in
a deeper knowledge and love of Mary of Nazareth."

Sr. Agnes Cunningham, S.S.C.M.
St. Mary of the Lake Seminary
Mundelein, Illinois

Letters from an Understanding Friend:
Jesus on the Way to Jerusalem

"Following Luke's version of Jesus' last journey to Jerusalem, Isaias Powers offers 40 reflective letters from the Lord. We are Jesus' confidants with whom he shares his feelings, problems, fears, sorrows, and depressions. Although Jesus' daily trials do not compare with the suffering of the crucifixion, Powers believes these small problems help him become more human. We come to realize that Jesus suffered as we are suffering and he can empathize with our feelings... The book offers a different way of looking at the last year of Jesus' life. Perfect for lenten meditation."

Spiritual Book News

Women of the Gospel: Sharing God's Compassion

"For once the silent women of the gospel speak out. Haven't you ever wanted to sneak up on them—Peter's mother-in-law, or the future mother-in-law at the marriage of Cana, or the sinful woman who washed Jesus' feet—and shout: 'Speak! Don't just stand there! Tell me what you are thinking'? Each of these women speaks to something—or someone—within ourselves: we all have our shy self, our left-out self, our embarrassed self, our sinful self.

"Each of us, whether man or woman, married or single, in-laws and out-laws, feels a bond with these women of the gospel, due to the perceptive sensitivity of Father Isaias."

Carroll Stuhlmueller, C.P.
Catholic Theological Union

Healing WORDS from JESUS

ISAIAS POWERS

TWENTY-THIRD PUBLICATIONS
Mystic, CT 06355

Twenty-Third Publications
185 Willow Street
P.O. Box 180
Mystic, CT 06355
(860) 536-2611
800-321-0411

ISBN 0-89622-682-4
Library of Congress Catalog Card Number 95-61867
Printed in the U.S.A.

Contents

HEALING WORDS FROM JESUS

Introduction

Imagine that you are at home one evening and the phone rings. It's an important person, you can gather, with a very important message. You *want* to hear what is being said, but it's very hard to do so . . . because you're standing right beside an open window, and just outside three men are working on the sidewalk with their jackhammers, and next to them two motorcyclists are revving up their bikes. So all you can hear is vroom . . . brrr, brrr . . . ack, ack . . . vroom, vroom . . . ack, ack, ack!

To make things worse, the whole family is having a big fight in the kitchen—everybody's yelling and screaming at one another. And in the room beside yours, the TV and radio are on full blast.

Now, how can *anybody* hear *anything* under those conditions?

It's not the fault of the important person on the other end of the line. *You* must do something to help the communication process by getting rid of the obstacles, removing as much of the noise clutter as you can. So, you close the window so the jackhammers and bikes don't sound so loud. You tell the people in the kitchen to stop shouting and you turn off the TV and radio. Now the phone message comes through clearly.

The moral of this scene is that we can help Jesus communicate with us by "de-obstaclizing" all those negative attitudes and noisy self-disclaimers that get in the way of really hearing and understanding him.

Jesus is all-powerful, and no one has more love, fuller truth, or greater wisdom. But while that is so, it's also true that Jesus has to rely on our cooperation in order to achieve his purposes of communicating his wisdom, healing our hurts, and sustaining and nourishing us. Just as the phone message couldn't be heard unless you did something about the noise coming from inside and outside your home, just so must we do something about these bad attitudes and irritable frustrations that hinder Jesus in his communication with us.

Over and over, Jesus has insisted that we be faithful to this work of "negating the negatives." Using many different parables and making his points in many different ways, the three "broken records" of our Lord were:

1. Don't judge! (That is, control the hurts in your memory; they deal with a past time that can never be reclaimed.)

2. Don't get discouraged! (That is, control all present-day moods of depression and discontent.)

3. Don't worry! (That is, control the tendency to fret about the future, which hasn't come yet.)

These pages explain how we can manage whatever bothersome attitudes hinder our growth. We *can* put these bullies under our control. Jesus says we *must*. It's all in knowing how to do it. This book is to help you formulate strategies for reducing the subversive activities within. It's all a matter of "closing the windows" to aggravations outside ourselves, calming the screaming anguish within, and turning off all those "interpretive TVs" (lodged in our brain) that get us down by broadcasting their bulletins of bitterness.

Note that I introduce most chapters with stories of real-life people who have allowed some obstacle or hindrance to enter their lives that prevented Christ's healing from reaching them. These stories are so true that they can be "true for everybody," one way or another. Of course, the individuals in the stories remain anonymous. May they help you to experience the healing power of Jesus.

1.

Joy as the
Starting Point

An Upbeat Way of Thinking About God

Let me tell you a story about a man who feels God is not kind but cruel. His anger with God goes back to the days when he served in the Korean War. Wounded seriously in the front lines, he was sent to the closest mobile army hospital. For many long and painful nights he suffered, and not too peacefully. The corporal usually in charge of the ward was overworked and very tired. So were the others who replaced him. "For God's sake" (they said to themselves—but really meant "For *our* sakes"), "we've got to get some rest. We can't listen to that guy crying in his pain all the time!" So they gave the man drugs so that they could get eight hours of uninterrupted sleep. As a result of the steady doses, the wounded man became addicted to the drugs, and for the next 25 years of his life had a craving for chemical peace!

Now it is many, many years since his wound healed, but his theology has not changed. He still thinks God is cruel and selfish, because a few army orderlies treated him as though he were a nobody. From that terrible ordeal in Korea, God has been colored by the same brush. Even today, whenever the man thinks about God, it is in terms of the monsters of the M.A.S.H. ward who told him, "We don't care about you. You're an obstacle to our night's rest. Get lost!"

How would you reason with this Korean veteran? How do you reason with yourself when something like this comes up in your life, people in authority who treated you poorly? This is an important question, because we all discover the value of ourselves and others in the value we put on God. That is, if we think God is mean and doesn't care about us, we assume that others feel the same, and sometimes we find ourselves not caring either. We think of God as a "generic monster" who caused all the bad experiences of our life. And we must admit, there has been a lot of that.

Parents, baby-sitters, older brothers and sisters, and teachers want to get some rest from a child's hyperactive "whys" and whines. They also want to strengthen their moral authority by using the imperatives of a powerful deity who is obviously on their side. Perhaps they have said something like the following, in the same mood of impatience manifested by the orderlies in the Korean hospital:

- You hit your baby brother—God will punish you for that.
- I'll tell Father how naughty you've been, and then you'll get it.
- You know how obedient the little boy Jesus was to his par-

ents. How sad you make him because you are not obedient to us.

• You fibbed! You'd better tell that in confession.
• Remember, angels are always watching you and they cry if you look at that part of your body.

So, God and all God's representatives become for the child a repository of power, something to fear. There are so few ways to please God, they think, but so many ways to disappoint. Little by little, it becomes an impossible task.

It's too bad these things happen. Nobody's perfect. (After all, the ones who have hurt us were stuck with *their* bad experiences, too!) However, we don't have to be under the spell of our bad memories forever. We can begin to understand that God is kind and caring if we let Jesus and his healing power be the starting point of our theology, instead of our association with all those bad experiences. If we take Jesus seriously, we can begin to understand God as a celebrating Father, instead of a critical orderly who'll do anything to get some sleep. With Jesus, we have celebration at its best.

Our Lord was forever revealing God as the jovial host of a great party *and* the heavenly caterer of happiness. Who could possibly be more festive than a person who is preparing a great marriage feast that will last forever? Indeed, God is so expansive in exuberance as to tell servants to go even to the out-of-the-way places and bring in everybody "so that my banquet hall will be filled!" (Matthew 22:1–14; Luke 14:16–24). And who could be more festive *and* forgiving than a merciful father of us prodigal sinners who embraces us and welcomes us to a magnificent homecoming party? (Luke 15:11–32)

Our Lord not only talked about his Father in terms of joy and a festive party; he also practiced what he preached. On one occasion he was positively thrilled with joy. The disciples were having a happy reunion. (One gets the impression it was very much like the locker room—champagne and all—of a baseball team that just won the World Series.) The 72 had just come back from their first road trip. They were successful. They had achieved. They had healed. Their words had been well received. Their God-given power to restore life was stronger than the devil's power to lead people into death and discouragement. It was a great feeling. They shared their enthusiasm and mission stories with the Lord and with one another (Luke 10:17–21).

At this point, St. Luke mentions that Jesus was "thrilled with joy." Celebrating the occasion with them, he praised them: "That's wonderful. I rejoice with you. And remember this—you are great, and my Father loves you not only for the good that you did, but also, and even more so, for the fact that you are my friends. Your names are written in the book of life." Then Jesus "rejoiced in the Holy Spirit and said: 'I offer you praise, O Father, Lord of heaven and earth, because what you have hidden from the learned and the clever you have revealed to the merest children. Yes, Father, you have graciously willed it so'" (Luke 10:21–22).

Then Jesus prayed. He was so filled with joy, he couldn't stop. We can imagine him saying, "Thanks to the joy of my disciples, I thank you, Father, for the wonderful love and life you give to all. I now have even more reason to praise you for your goodness."

Isn't this a lovely idea? We can think of all the normal times that give us reason to celebrate: a child getting a good report card, a wedding, a woman giving birth, a priest being ordained, someone being promoted or praised, a person being loved, a home team winning the championship. These and a thousand more are all ways of coming together with friends and saying, "Good! We're pretty good, aren't we?" And when this happens, it provides the occasion for Jesus to rejoice.

Life has been celebrated. Love and gratitude and care have been proclaimed. Jesus ratifies our natural loyalties and tells us again that we are worthwhile, and should continue to celebrate. Then he gives the deepest reason: ". . . do not rejoice so much in the fact that devils are subject to you as that your names are inscribed in heaven" (Luke 10:20).

Jesus could add, thanks to our joy, that he has even more reason to be grateful and to praise his Father for the wonderful ways wisdom and love are bestowed on little ones. Thinking this way is a far cry from thinking of God as a cranky critic who isn't pleased with anything.

There is a better way to begin. We start with our own joy. This develops in us a sense of accomplishment, a feeling of self-worth. We share these with our Lord, as his first friends did, and he heals us as he healed them. Then Jesus is further stimulated to increase his joy, to praise our friendship, and to thank his Father. Finally, we can relish-by-anticipation the great party in heaven where temporary joys will be furthered to unimaginable limitlessness.

2.

Joined to Christ

Discovering the Inside Stuff of Love

Suppose you and two other people are in the waiting room of a psychiatrist's office. This is the first time for the three of you. While you are waiting, the doctor suggests a simple assignment. Having made certain that you all know who Jesus is, and that you respect him, she asks you to write two paragraphs, one on "Who is Jesus?" and one on "What are the most important things Jesus did and said?"

Before the doctor returns, you share your stories. A woman, wistfully sad, remembers how differently Jesus approached the sinners of his time. "Gently and sweetly and without raised voice," she said. "'Jesus would forgive everybody everything. He would let people just be as they want to be."

A man, on the other hand, remembered Jesus making whips and throwing money lenders out of the temple and demanding that everyone be perfect as God is perfect. What was real to this man was the way Jesus castigated the power structure of the Pharisees—that decadent "in group"—and told everyone in no uncertain terms that they had better shape up!

What was your response? How do you see the significance of Jesus Christ?

Most people, it seems, like to think of Jesus as a kind of "divine sanction," or support, of the peculiar turn of personality that they already have: "I am like this—and it's okay because so is Jesus." (Which means: "I am an angry revolutionary; so is Jesus." Or "I am too lazy to change my compulsions; I just want to be for-given-in-to. So why can't people do for me what Jesus did?")

This tendency to treat Christ with our own prepackaged bias is very difficult to overcome. One danger with this can be called the "puppy dog syndrome," turning the situation around. God is the dog and should obey us. Does a dog challenge its owner? It simply obeys and applauds the biases of behavior that already exist, benignly wagging its tail.

But Jesus will not live in our hearts unless he is permitted to turn all our thinking, attitudes, and behavior topsy-turvy. He will change us and heal us, taking the initiative in our lives. We will not change him or dress him up in our likeness as though he were an uncomplaining, doll-like prince of peace. Our role is to listen, not to dictate. Our responsibility is to embrace everything he tells us, not to simplify his revelation by quoting passages acceptable to us and discarding what is uncomfortable.

Hence, if our temperament is one that gets angry quickly, the indignation of Jesus should not be so well remembered as his gentleness and his patient love. But if our personality is one that gets lazy quickly or is afraid to act for fear of being criticized by worldly people, it would be well to ponder his indignation and to remember the uncompromising challenges he puts to us.

If we don't let Jesus give balance to our lives, we are making God's revelation subservient to us. In the preceding chapter, we saw that God can become a fiction of our own imagination because of certain dramatic—sometimes traumatic—experiences in our past life. This chapter deals with the more ordinary and humdrum stuff. Because most of our "everydays" are unspectacular, they can go unnoticed. Even so, they can add up to a very unnerving amalgam of ill will; and, as such, they can present to our subconscious a terrible prejudice against God.

The spiritual and psychological dynamic goes like this:

- Mom neglected me when she kept talking on the telephone instead of paying attention to me.
- Dad disapproved of me when I didn't get straight A's in school.
- My older brother and sister were often too busy with their own affairs to bother with me.
- My family ignored my enthusiasms and belittled my self-doubts.
- My friends at school often razzed me (too short/too fat, long nose/pug nose, big ears/four eyes, acne/accent). And they also warned me that I'd be "out of it" unless I acted just like the rest of them.
- So much of my life was threatened with "You'd better behave, or else you'll get it!"

And so it goes. Other mean characters enter the story as the person ages: the boss, the neighbors, fellow workers, play-ground bullies, village gossips, pastors, bureaucrats, doctors, orderlies, etc.

Then God comes on the scene. The usual routine is to put God "out there" with the others: Mom at her most uncaring times, Dad at his most disapproving, family at their most pre-occupied, friends at their most threatening. Out of all this mix of unhappy memories, God becomes "The Great Disapproving, Rejecting, Belittling Meany" who is either 1) too busy to be bothered with me, or 2) full of imperious threats, warning me, "You'd better behave, or else you'll get it!" ("It," in this case, means the most frightening weapons in the arsenal of fear: bad luck, ill health, death, and the doom of hell.)

Many people, to a greater or lesser extent, think of God this way. They first of all relive how all the "big people" in their past have hurt them, rejected them, or—worst of all—ignored them, leaving them feeling only marginally meaningful. Then they plunk God into this reawakened past and blow God up into some kind of mysterious "corporate other"—as bad as all the others were at their worst.

Now we come to Jesus and his topsy-turvy revelation of the Father. This is where his true genius shines. He tells us to make a 180-degree shift in our thinking. We are not to base our ideas on what the Father is like by what we have seen of vin-dictive people (even fathers and mothers) around us. Jesus is the only Son the Father has, and it is *he* who tells us who the Father is.

To understand the Father, we must wash out of our hearts all the hurts that are still there as a result of other people's meanness and our own. We must fill our hearts with good thoughts, good memories of ourselves. We ought to focus our thoughts on those times when we were at our best, listening with an understanding heart to someone, helping a friend with advice or money, being faithful to a loved one who was trying to pull through sickness or depression, enlivening a party, forgiving those who hurt us, offering strength to the weak and hope to the doubting.

We can imagine Jesus saying:

You know how imperfect you are. You are not good listeners, or strong, or helpful, all the time. But sometimes you are. And when you, imperfect as you are, live at your best and love at your very best—this is the clue to the right understanding of my Father.

Maybe your own parents [teachers, bosses] did not seem to care about you, lost in their own preoccupations. My Father is not like that. My Father is like you when you do care about your loved ones—only he is even better than you at your best.

Maybe you were made to feel small and left out by others, and this is why you have such beautiful compassion for those who are down and out. My Father is not like those who hurt your feelings. He is like you at your most compassionte moments—only he is even more so.

The clue to understanding is here. Both Matthew and Luke recorded it in my gospel. The figures of speech are not too difficult to grasp. I said, and say it still (see Matthew 7:7–11; Luke 11:11–13):

"If a little one asks for bread,
will you give him a stone?
Or if he asks for a fish,
will you give him a scorpion?
. . . Therefore if you, imperfect as you are,
know how to give good gifts to your little ones,

how much more
will your Father give good things
to those who ask him."

Please don't use those hurts (the "stones") you received from others as the way to understand who my
Father is. Use the good memories of yourself, the times
you've given the "bread" of kindness and patient care to
others, as the lens by which you see how God is kind to
you.

In a way, this essay deals with prayer, about the right attitude to have in your relationship with God. It approaches the
subject negatively, suggesting two important attitudes *not* to
have. God will do the rest. The Father will send his Spirit to
nurture us into the love and joy experienced by Jesus—as long
as we don't "me-first" him.

As long as we 1) do not try to simplify Jesus' message to suit
our needs or fashion his personality according to our pre-
conceptions, and 2) as long as we think of the Father in terms
of *us at our best*, not *others at their worst*, then we will have the
strong gentleness of Jesus, and can be called a Christian after
his own heart.

We will love our Father much more confidently too. We'll
learn to be grateful for the bread he gives us and be alert for
more opportunities to give bread to others, so that we can understand God's kindness even better than before.

3.

God's Thoroughness With Love

"Nourishing as the Sun, Gentle as the Rain"

Suppose you are at the airport, waiting for your flight. You are reading Matthew's Gospel, the Sermon on the Mount (5:43–48). A momentary flash of fright comes over you as you read Christ's command "You must be perfect, as your heavenly Father is perfect!" Two people sitting near notice the change in your mood. They suspect that you have just received some very bad news. You show them the Gospel passage, without comment. After a time, the woman responds:

If Jesus tells us that we have to be perfect, then I don't

have a chance! I am far from perfect! Everyone has always told me that. Speaking with all the self-assurance of
God, they have hammered it home to me that, "If a thing
is worth doing, it's worth doing perfectly!" I haven't
done anything perfectly. At no time could I have said that
a day could not have been better, a deed could not have
been improved, a motive could not have been nobler, a
thought could not have been clearer, a thing-worth-doing
could not have taken more careful preparation. I despair,
ever, of becoming perfect. And so I despair of God.

Coming from an entirely different perspective, but messing
up Christ's meaning just as much, the other, a man, said:

Oh, that's where that saying came from. I knew Jesus told
everybody to be perfect, but I didn't know where it was
in the Gospel. Now I've got some real ammunition! You
see, I've been on my family's case for years. Jesus told us
to be perfect. That is the natural expectation. Well, my
family is not perfect. Neither is my work group, or my
community, or my neighbors, or my parents, or my parish. None of them! So I'm justified in treating all of them
with nagging and dissatisfaction because that's the way
Jesus is prepared to treat them!

Whew! These two individuals represent us all, at times. The
spirit of perfectionism can either freeze us into demoralized in-
activity or boil us over with hot-tempered criticism. It leads to
such typical family comments as:

•Dad, Dad, I finally did it—I got a 98 in math this semester.
  (Response: What happened to the other two points?)

- My husband snores. How can I live with a man who snores?
- My wife gets tired sometimes after supper. She never did 30 years ago. . . .What's wrong with her?
- I thought, when I entered religious life, that it was a state of perfection. The people I live with are still far from it!
- Some priests still smoke cigarettes, after all the surgeon general has said!
- I'll take no advice from those two people. They have faults; they don't always practice what they preach! So any good ideas they might have are irrevocably blemished by their imperfections.

Much of the modern "demand for faultlessness/discovery of fault/despair of the faulty one" sequence stems from a fascination with machines and a desire to make machines out of people. It is a sickness in society. It is true that a machine has to be perfect or it is not good at all. If only one of the thousands of parts of the spacecraft does not work, the rocket will not reach the moon. If one gear breaks down in the hydroelectric plant, the whole city falls into darkness. If a scientist forgets one little step, the laboratory experiment is all wrong.

But from all this, it does not follow that the boy is not smart because he got one out of 50 problems wrong, that Babe Ruth is a failure because he struck out so often, that a girl is a "bad girl" because she's done a bad thing.

People are not machines. If the battery of a car goes bad, the car is bad; it doesn't work. So the mechanic files down the rust on the battery terminal (a kind of "automotive nagging"), concentrating on what's wrong; then the car is ready to roll.

But people can't be fixed by nagging and concentrating on the faulty area. And we can't junk people as we do old cars, leaving them in some abandoned heap to rust, while we go out and get another model. This is what often happens, though: either constant nagging about what is wrong or junking the person altogether. The strange thing is that many people who behave this way use Jesus as their authority: "Didn't our Lord command us to be perfect?"

Yes, he did. However, when Jesus told us this, he had a particular meaning in mind. The call to be perfect was at the end of a long series of instructions. Consequently, the meaning Jesus gives the word "perfect" was flavored and explained by all that went before it, and especially by two extremely important symbols—sun and rain—which make his way of saying "Be perfect" completely contrary to our modern perfectionism.

The fullest version of Christ's "explanation" is in Matthew 5:43–48. One can tell, by the way Jesus warms up to the subject, that a case is not being built up advocating behavior that would nag other people or lead oneself to despair: "You have heard the commandment, 'You shall love your neighbor but hate your enemy.' My command to you is: love your enemies; pray for your persecutors" (43–44).

Another version is: "Love those who tell lies about you." Obviously, Jesus is talking about long-suffering and forgiveness and patience. How, then, can this passage be the excuse for so much short-tempered "short-suffering" of other people's faults and such impatience with our own? Then the beautiful metaphors appear: "This will prove that you are of your heavenly Father, for his sun rises on the bad and the good; he rains on the just and the unjust" (5:45).

The sun and the rain, the two necessary conditions of all life. Without them, we have no grass, no seed, no trees, no shade, no flowers, no eggs, no lamb chops, no water, no wood, no sunsets, no rainbows—no life at all.

God the Father is thorough with gifts, with these two gifts in particular. All share and share alike. God does not cause anyone to die or dry up for lack of the bare essentials. God, who is not snobbish or punishing or impatient, does not say, "You farmers are lazy; so no more sun and rain on your acres! I'm reserving my love only for the good guys." Or, "Stay hungry and thirsty, you dishonest people; I'm cutting you off from your source of supply! Without sun and rain, nothing will grow and then you'll be sorry for all your faults (nyaah, nyahh)!" God does not act this way. Jesus told us so.

Then our Lord continues, in a familiar homespun style: "If you love only those who love you, what merit is there in that? Do not tax collectors do as much? And if you greet only your brothers and sisters, what is so praiseworthy about that? Do not pagans do as much?" (5:46–48)

With all his easy manner of reasoning, Jesus' message is serious and dramatic. We must be exceptional in this matter of "giving sun and rain" to others and to ourselves. It is an extremely difficult response-ability, but we must live up to it if we want to be followers of Christ.

Then comes the bombshell, our Lord's concluding remark: "In a word, you must be perfect as your heavenly Father is perfect."

St. Luke (6:36) quotes Jesus as saying, in the same context, "Be compassionate as your Father is compassionate." Both evangelists mean the same. This teaching is the opposite of perfectionism. If I get down on others because they talk behind my back, or if I nag them for their blemishes of character, or if I mope because they are ungrateful for the good I do them; if I do any of these things, I am effectively withholding the necessities of life from them, refusing to give them "sun and rain," without which there is no growth.

And if I let depression get its hold on me and wallow in self-pity because of my own imperfections, I'm acting contrary to the Father's way of working things out with me.

God patiently sends sunshine and gentle rain to get us to grow again. Often we don't let it happen. We close the shutters to the sun and stifle ourselves in self-inflicted drought. Yes, we love ourselves when we've had a good day or have done a good job or have seen everything run smoothly. But, to paraphrase our Lord, "So what! That's not exceptional. Even pagans do that much. You become a real Christian when you are patient with yourself, even on bad days, when faults are obvious and tears are imminent and life is dreary. That is when the test case comes!" Jesus tells us:

You must be thorough as my Father is thorough. You must not withhold—from self or from others—the sun of gentleness and the soft rain of patient kindness. Even though the world is blemished (as you are, too), you must continue to bestow, unconditionally, all those things (symbolized by sun and rain) that are needed for the God-given growth of others—and your God-giving growth.

4.

When You're Rejected

Healing's Need for Rest

Let us start with the Story of a Broken Arm:

A boy had just got a new bike and in his fresh enthusiasm sped too fast around a curve, fell, and broke his arm. Now, it would be unproductive for this eight-year-old to do nothing but moan and wince each time he touched it: "Ouch, it hurts. See? Whenever I put pressure on it . . . Ooo, it hurts so much!" But this is not helping his arm.

It would be just as ridiculous for the boy's parents only to analyze the cause of the problem: "I know why your arm hurts. It hurts because you broke it. You broke it because you fell off the bike. You fell off the bike because you weren't careful. You weren't careful because you didn't listen to us. You never do. If we told you once, we told you a thousand times (nag, nag, nag)." This may be an accurate description of the situation, but it is not helping the boy's arm.

What do good parents do? They take him to a doctor. The doctor does not do the healing—not directly. The doctor simply knows how to give the arm rest. He puts it in a cast. It is from the *inside* that healing takes place. The bone, once rested, mends itself. Then the muscles, little by little, build up again. And after a while, the arm is as good as new.

A broken arm is one thing: As soon as it is in a cast, it has no choice but to heal. Enforced casing makes for immobility and immobility allows for healing. But what happens to parts of us that can't be treated in the same way as the arm? Say you have a pimple on the tip of your tongue or a sore on the roof of your mouth. What do you do? What do we all do? We irritate the wound. We keep checking it out "to see if it's still there." Yes, it's still there! Indeed, we do the very thing that prevents the healing from taking place. We bear down on it!

When the pain is even further inside us, we often behave even more unwisely. What happens when someone betrays us, rejects us, denies our love or friendship, refuses to follow our advice? What happens when we betray ourselves, deny the best part of us because of our own sin or carelessness?

What happens? We do precisely what is best calculated to keep healing from taking place. Instead of putting the hurts of our heart "in a cast" and letting the scars mend themselves, we irritate the wound and keep checking on ourselves to see if it's still there.

We keep analyzing the situation, making an airtight case for ourselves as though we were a prosecuting attorney. As we brood over incident after incident, we could even give the case a name: "My Justification for Being Hurt." Once the case is prepared, we play the role to the hilt and turn friends and acquaintances into a mock jury who must listen—over and over again—to the case of "self against that member of my family," or "self against the boss."

Whether my "case against so-and-so" is justified or unjustified is not the point. To insist on one's "*right* to be hurt" makes as much sense as insisting on one *right* to be bothered by a pimple on the tip of the tongue, or the little boy's *right* to say "ouch" because he has a broken arm. A person's rights should not be the consideration in these cases. *Healing* must be the only thing that matters. Common sense joins Christ's command, and both are joined by the sound advice of the medical profession: We heal a broken heart the same way we heal a broken arm—give it rest.

This is easy enough to say, but not so easy to do. People's self-interest programs and their sometimes instinctive desire to exercise control get in the way of healing the hurts of the heart. Years ago, the comic strip "Peanuts" presented a fascinating scenario about all this. Crabby Lucy is dictating terms of behavior to Snoopy, the defenseless dog: "Charlie Brown has asked me to take care of feeding you today." Then she moves in for her bid to control Snoopy: "You know what this means, don't you? It means I have you in my *power!* I've had enough of your insults. You'd better behave today, because I control the supper dish. I've got you where I want you!" She concludes philosophically: "The hand that controls the supper dish rules the world!"

"Controlling the supper dish" is diabolical but it is efficient. It is used because it controls others to behave the way we want them to. Even little children learn to use it. I remember, when I was a little boy, saying, "Why, Mom? Why can't I stay up to listen to Fibber McGee and Molly? Joe Wilber's mother lets *him* stay up, and Carl Peglow's and Fred Fleishman's and the other guys' . . ."

See what I was doing? Implied in my nagging was the statement: "Unless you let me do what I want, I'm going to make you feel that you are not as good a mother as Joe Wilber's or the other boys'!" Sometimes I got my way by using the most efficient manipulation tool I had. Some instinct told me that nobody wants to feel "not as good as" someone else.

Parents use this manipulation on their children:

- Why can't you get as good grades as your sister?
- Why didn't you make the first team? Your friend did and he doesn't have the talent you do!
- Why can't you be in on time? You cause us more worry than all your brothers and sisters do!
- Why can't you obey us as Jimmy obeys his parents?

Teenagers use it, too: "Why can't I stay out until two? Everybody else does!" Parents respond with "I don't care about everybody else. You're not 'everybody else.'" Then the teens reply, "Then why do I get 'everybody else' thrown at me when you want me to be as neat as Brian, or as practical, or as brainy, or as popular?"

It's a vicious circle. Spouse to spouse applies the same system of "manipulation by comparison":

- Why can't you make more money or take me out more often? Your brother treats his wife better than you treat me!
- Why can't you balance the checkbook the way our neighbor Sally does?
- Sure I'm going out again. None of my friends' wives nag their husbands about it!

And so it goes. To understand why this system is so efficient, go back to poor Snoopy being threatened with the empty supper dish. Consider the dog as everybody and consider the supper dish as unsatisfied needs. Then take these needs out of the physical realm and into the psychological. What are they? They are the needs we have to live a life that is both meaningful and productive. They are the hunger we have to be good for others—to feel deep down that "I'm okay. I'm somebody, and appreciated as such. In my own right, I am good as a child (a parent, a spouse, a fellow worker, a neighbor, a friend). The people in my life are happy that I am who I am; I make their world better by my presence."

Everyone has these huge appetites. They could be summed up in the most basic need of all: the need to feel worthwhile. If this is so, other people can threaten us with comparison ethics by using "supper dish control." We are in their power, if they use this ploy. We are very likely to flinch if they say: "You'd better behave according to my dictates, or I won't feed you with the acceptance you hunger for—and you'll have to go to bed without your supper! I can make you feel *un*worthwhile by comparing you unfavorably with someone else. You may be miserable but I'll get you to give in!"

After some years of such a starvation diet, it becomes almost second nature to keep irritating ourselves with our "unworthwhileness." We begin to do it to ourselves: "I'm not as good (or as smart, or as pretty, or as successful, or as happy, or as healthy) as the others." Then, because we've gone so long without nourishment, it becomes difficult to take in any solid food. When we are praised or productive or promoted or appreciated, these touches of worthwhileness go unheeded. We just cannot believe we're any good at all.

It is no wonder, then, that it is very difficult to put a cast on the hurts of the heart. Like the little boy with the broken arm who keeps saying "Ouch, Ouch. Every time I move it, it hurts," we tend to keep comparing ourselves to others who seem to be, somehow, better off.

It is time to stop this nonsense of operating out of the control syndrome, comparing people to others (which is the activity most likely to aggravate their hurts) and and to stop letting others work their manipulative tricks on us.

It is time, instead, to pray this prayer for self-improvement:

I am wrong, and it is sinful to nag others by comparing them unfavorably to someone else. Even though it is the quickest way of punishing them and the most efficient way of getting what I want from them, I won't do it any more.

And I won't nag myself any more, either. That's not the way to be healed of my hurts. It won't help to keep irritating the wounds or wishing I were as good as ____. I'll give myself, and others, rest. I'll let the mending come from the inside, with the sun and rain, the love and peace, that are available to me now from God and from the worthy—and "worthwhiling"—friends I have.

5.

When People
Snub You

Christ's "Sun" and "Rain" Revisited

"Humph" is a sound we utter when we are at our worst. It captures us, like a candid camera, right at the point where we begin to punish somebody else with silent treatment. There is a toss of the head, a curl of scorn on the mouth, a turn of the shoulder in the other direction . . . and an ugly guttural expression that sounds something like "humph!"

Perhaps we don't realize the effects we have on others when we treat them with disdain; but we certainly know how we feel when someone hurts us this way. The direct opposite of love is not anger or criticisms, or war or teasing, or sarcasm. The enemy most oppressive is *silence*, that unspoken sweep of attitudes that clearly indicates, "You are not worth talking to, or being with, or anything. You are worthy only of contempt!"

Observe your own behavior over the past few years when you responded to someone who was important to you—friend, fellow worker, family—and who was somehow insulting or insensitive. There are really only four ways to react, and *continue* to react, to that situation. Notice how often you have favored option 2 or 3.

1. Greet the individual warmly and shake his hand: "Hail fellow, well met." (We can't do that; we are still smarting from his hurt.)

2. Stay on the same side of the street and punch him in the nose or give him verbal abuse so that he will never forget what he did to you. (Of course, this offers him no choice but to remain your enemy forever.)

3. Put our nose in the air and walk over to the other side of the street. (Treat him as a nobody—refuse him the sun and rain of mercy, aborting all chance of reconciliation.)

4. Stay on the same side of the street and simply say hello, smile if you can manage it, and mention some innocuous thing like the weather. You could even be open to an inspiration that suggests getting together later on. (Maybe. At least it is a possibility.)

Option 4 is the only healthy one. The person who has hurt you may be a member of the family, a fellow worker giving you a bad time, a friend who turned on you, or a pesty neighbor. You probably cannot embrace him as though nothing happened. But you cannot claim the right to banish him or anyone to non-existence. Jesus commanded us to be like the Father "who does not exclude anyone from the gifts of sun and rain." In the most practical terms, that means, "Don't punish anyone with the silent treatment!"

Our Lord does not demand the impossible. But he does tell us that we must be at least "better than average" in our behavior. Those who aren't Christian retaliate severely when they are hurt—an eye for an eye, a tooth for a tooth, a silence returned for a silence imposed, insult for insult, deep freeze for a deep hurt—but Christians must behave differently. They cannot break down the possibilities for growth or stifle all future chances for reconciliation.

Dr. Carl Rogers has an excellent, insightful analysis of unproductive, as opposed to helpful, behavior. He calls such behavior "that which puts other people on the defensive," that which brings out the worst in others. We would call unproductive behavior *sins*, offenses and negligences against our neighbor.

There are four principal ways we bring out the worst in people:

1. by judging them;
2. by trying to manipulate them;
3. by acting superior to them;
4. by treating them as though they didn't exist.

The first method of unproductive behavior is a form of *evaluation*; whenever we judge someone, assess her motives, assume we "know what makes her tick," we trigger defense mechanisms in her. Description, instead of evaluation, is a better way to communicate. (This will be discussed in the next chapter.)

The second method, *control*, has already been discussed in Chapter 4. Whenever our main concern is to manipulate others ("Why can't you be as good as . . . ?") we should expect them to feel used. Once they feel used, they'll be defensive and act "unproductively" against us.

The third method is called *emphasizing superiority*. This happens whenever we keep harping on what makes us better than someone else—"I'm older." Or "I'm younger." Or "I'm the boss." Or "I've had more experience." Or "I've had more schooling." Or "I know the ropes." Or "I've been sick longer." Or "When I was your age, I walked to school and had it tough and really had to work"—whenever any such superiority is emphasized, the intent is to put the other person down, make him feel inferior, bring out the worst in him. Sensing equality brings out the best in others, but constant references to "what makes me better than you" bring out their defensive behavior. (This, too, will be taken up in detail later.)

The last, and the most deadly, of these behavior sins is something that is rarely considered when we make an examination of conscience. Dr. Rogers even has a clumsy word for it: *neutrality* as opposed to *empathy*. Neutrality is what I call the "silent treatment," reducing someone to a nobody, relegating a person to the world of non-entity. The deadliest sin of all! Yet it is so often excused: "I didn't *do* anything. I didn't *say* anything." True enough. You did not throw stones. But you refused to give bread. You neglected to bestow "sun and rain," without which there is no growth.

What is the most oppressive kind of punishment, after all? Is it not silent treatment? Isn't the threat of exclusion the most devastating among teenagers or any peer group? Isn't "not speaking to each other" the last step in a marriage break-up?

Neutrality is the opposite of love. To reduce anybody to "nothing of importance" closes off all further chance for a meaningful relationship. There is a way for every other hurt to be healed; there is no way for a nobody to become a somebody again. Humpty Dumpty has crashed on the cold shoulder, and all the king's horses and all the king's men can't put Humpty back together again.

Empathy is different. It is what religion calls charity, what our Lord describes as "not refusing the sun and rain to anyone," even though they are dishonest, ungrateful, or insulting. Empathy charges us to do for others what we would want them to do for us and keep communication lines open—even though we cannot turn the other cheek as yet. Empathy does not one-sidedly close off the possibility of a change of heart.

Empathy is Jesus Christ who, even though Simon Peter denied him publicly, rose from the dead and stayed on Simon's side of the street and offered him a second chance: "Peace be with you." Jesus gained a friend he could easily have punished by silent treatment. Empathy is the sun and the rain making it possible for peace to exist and love to grow in those relationships where there were only hot blusterings and cold silences before.

6.

Peacekeeping Responsibilities

Being Personally Important

An older priest told me this story while we were giving a parish mission. It was his custom, he said, to surprise a certain type of penitent with a twofold penance: "Whenever anyone says in confession, 'Bless me, Father, because I have sinned. I got angry at my husband because he did this and that to me. I got impatient with the children because they behaved this way and that . . .' I would say, at the end, 'Well, ma'am, for *your* sins say one Hail Mary, and for your *family's* sins say three rosaries.'" The point is simple enough. The woman was not confessing her own sins. She was justifying her anger and indignation. It was her husband's sins, and her children's, that she was confessing.

Seldom, though, does anyone speak this way in confession. Almost always the mood of communication is personal sorrow and the style is *first person singular*: "*I* have done wrong; *I* am sorry."

Before I was ordained, I used to wonder what would happen to me after I started hearing confessions. Optimistic by nature, I wondered if I would change after listening to people, hour upon hour, admit the seamy side of their lives: their selfishness and cowardice and sins. Would I turn into a pessimist and lose hope in people once I opened myself to this avalanche of wrongdoing?

As a matter of fact, the opposite is true. As a priest for 35 years and the instrument of Christ's mercy in this sacrament for thousands of people, I have been privileged to experience people at their very best, at their most honest and sincere. They speak in the first person singular. Considering the difficulties they are up against—temptations to sin, situations that so readily lead to frustration and impatience, so many reasons for despairing—I marvel at their courage and resilience. I thank God for the goodness I see in those who accept forgiveness and new life again. Hearing confessions is such a positive experience.

Everyone has had this good feeling at times. It's usually a one-to-one communication with a trusting friend, perhaps at the kitchen table. The friend will be honest and specific, instead of guarded and vague. They use the first person, not the second: "I," not "you."

That's the personal, confessional side of my ministry. At other times, though—with individual counselling or group discussions—the turn of the conversation is quite different. Very often (especially at first) personal responsibility is shrouded by the use of the second person, "you." This way, the blame for the world's ills are put squarely on the shoulders of "other people" who are not present.

Certain typical phrases keep repeating themselves. They sound something like these:

- You can't seem to communicate with your kids any more!
- You shudder when you think about what's going in songs and movies!
- You try to explain things to your wife (husband), but she (he) just won't listen to you.

I try to suggest that *some* wives do listen, *some* husbands are thoughtful. Not everyone has the same poor degree of communication skills. So why use the vague pronoun "you" that places everybody in one basket . . . and deftly gets the speaker off the hook. ("It's *your* fault, and everybody else's fault; I, personally, am not involved in the assessment.")

I plead with the people (and with myself): "Take responsibility for your own feelings. Instead of saying 'You don't communicate with me,' say 'We aren't communicating very well; how can we improve?'"

The same principles apply to domestic problems and workplace problems, too. The deadly "you" ends up with a shrug of the shoulders and a fatalistic sigh: "What can you do?" means "What can *anyone* do!" means "Nothing can be done!" The word "I" prepares for a personal challenge; the word "We" begins to probe new possibilities: "What can *we* do . . . ?"

This is the first way of using the "deadly you"; it is when the word, in all honesty, should be "I." It goes unnoticed most of the time; yet it is deadly because it drains off personal responsibility. As long as the feeling remains—"What can you do?"—the implied message is "I can't do anything about it because it is everybody's fate!" The "you" intones a defeatist attitude; that's what makes it so deadly.

The second "deadly you" is more obvious. It is the "evaluate you" that Carl Rogers described as the expression that is bound to bring out defensive and unproductive behavior in other people. Not only Carl Rogers, but Jesus himself warns us over and over, "Do not judge, lest you be judged."

Evaluating other people's motives, meanings, or mistakes is judging. It assumes that I know the inside working of another person's character.

- You hate me!
- You don't love me any more!
- You are deliberately avoiding my question!
- You are boring!

What comeback does the other person have? Either to admit, "Yes, you are right. I am no good." Or to retaliate by making an evaluative statement right back:

- If you would only change, then I wouldn't hate you so much!
- I didn't start the cold war. You did!
- You always avoid my questions. How do you like it when somebody else dishes it out to you?
- I'm not boring. You're the one who's too preoccupied to listen!

And the "battle of the pointed finger" is underway. Both sides lose, of course. Nobody wins. It wasn't meant to be a win-lose game, but it turned out to be just that.

It is easy to point the finger, to play the game of "you." No risk is taken. The person called "I" is the cool cat: disengaged, uninvolved, pointing out what is wrong with the person called "you." The image is that of a comfortable and protected television booth, high above the stands, protected from the noise and dirt of the football field; the judgmental "finger pointer" is the cool commentator expressing criticism of the errant players moving around in the game of life below.

A more honest way of communicating has the word "I" sprinkled liberally all over. "I feel unloved"; "I feel avoided"; "I am bored." Then dialogue can go somewhere. There is a difference between "I am bored" and "you are boring." It may be that I am tired at the moment, or preoccupied, or uninterested in that particular subject. None of these has anything to do with the other individual. Another likelihood is that perhaps he is boring to me, but not to others. There are a number of possibilities, but they are all closed off by the pointed-finger statement, "You are boring!"

The "you" approach is safer, though. If I say "I am bored," I run the risk of discovering that the fault is as much mine as it is his. Then I am no longer safe in the TV booth; I'm down on the playing field myself.

Dr. Rogers tells this story on himself. (It is more difficult to practice this than preach it.) One night, at the end of a party, he and his wife quarreled. They were angry at each other. The wife was driving, too fast for safety, over a wet, winding road. He was afraid of an accident. Ordinarily, he would have pretended to be the detached observer, coolly pointing out—using the "you" approach—what was wrong with her: "You're angry, aren't you! You don't care whether we skid or not! Typical woman driver—taking your anger out on a poor car!" Then she would have replied: "You're always criticizing my driving! Didn't you take your anger out on the poor car when you slammed the door?" And another fight would have developed in earnest.

This time, though, he decided to practice what he preached. He decided to describe his feelings, rather than evaluate her behavior, using the "I" approach: "Honey, I'm scared to go this fast over a slippery road." It was risky for him to put it this way. All she had to do was go faster or stay at the same speed. This would be the most effective way of saying, by implication, "I don't care about your feelings. You don't count!" It would have hurt. Actually (though she was still too angry to talk as yet) she did slow down. This made him feel good. He was loved. She cared by responding to his honest description of his feelings.

It is riskier to be personal than to be judgmental, as I have said. We make ourselves vulnerable to a rebuke, or, worse, the silent rebuff of a shrug that says, "I don't care how you feel." It is difficult to be honest about our feelings and take a chance of being hurt again; but it is the only way love can grow and communication lines can stay open.

Jesus could have "played it cool." Late in the evening of Holy Thursday, he could have said, "I don't need anybody. You men are not really my friends. You don't even care enough to stay with me, even to stay awake. Well, it doesn't matter. I'm tough! I can go it alone!" Of course, our Lord said nothing of the sort. He simply described how he felt and what he needed . . . and waited for their response. The apostles heard him clearly: "Please stay awake with me. Pray with me. I need you. It will strengthen me to know that I can count on you." This is the message, as the words came out, right from the heart.

And their reaction? They promptly fell asleep. "Their hearts were heavy," St. Luke tells us. The apostles disclaimed Christ's

claim on them because "We're having troubles of our own!"
This hurt, even more so because Jesus already admitted he
needed them. Even so, he stayed true to himself and did not
pretend that he was not sad.

After Easter, Jesus, of course, remembered how his friends
had let him down. The Sunday of Resurrection was only four
days after the time when the Eleven went to sleep, then ran
away, and one of them denied him. If Jesus were a lesser man,
he would have demanded revenge . . . a certain groveling in
the dust! He would have been justified if he chose to rub their
noses in their own sins, and tell them that they couldn't be
trusted, and say, "I told you so!"

Jesus didn't stoop to such small-minded judgmentalisms.
Instead, he gave these imperfect disciples the best gift of all:
complete forgiveness and his promise of peace: "Peace be with
you," he told them. Then he spoke these overwhelming words
of mercy (John 20:21): "Just as the Father has sent me (with all
the confidence and trust that I could do a good job of love), I
send you into the world with the same confidence and trust.
You can do it!" Imagine that! Less than a week ago, these men
proved they couldn't be counted on . . . and here was Jesus en-
trusting them with the whole God-movement we call the
church!

How amazing that Jesus should treat us with such cordial-
ity, such confidence, such grace.

A Christian is one who lives as Christ did while on earth,
one who radiates "lively talk," keeping open the lines of communication, making it possible for forgiveness to have a
chance to grow.

An enemy of Christ—an *un*christian—is one who uses the
tactic of silent treatment or either one of the two deadly
"yous." The sun is filtered out with remembered hurts; the

growth-giving rain is refused with a *humph* and an upturned nose. And nothing happens because the soil is dry. Jesus has no place to give judger or judged the peace that is his alone to give.

The gift of peace is his, but the decision to let this peace take root is ours. The choice depends on how we use the shrugged shoulder, the pointed finger, the sometimes deadly word called *you*.

7.

Controlling the Need to Control

We're Not God

The main character in this story is Snow White, as we know her from the Walt Disney version of the folk tale, which draws from sources far back in history, before there was a written word, when grandmothers of the world told this story to their grandchildren so that they would grow up well.

There is a bit of Snow White in us all, young and old, male and female. The lessons to be learned are sensitive considerations, not easy to understand because they call upon the complex and demanding art of "How to Be Good and to Do Good." This is what the story skillfully deals with. Let's see, how does it start?

Once there was this good, hard-working, put-upon girl (read you and me, of whatever age or sex). She fled from a fearful situation (in her case, the home of a wicked stepmother; in our case, it could be almost anything). She was with friends, the seven little men; and she was happy enough just taking care of the cottage. But she had a dream that some day her prince would come and change her life into perfect happiness (dreams such as we all have, on way or another).

So much for the setting. Now comes the experience with the devil. Two devils in this case—one, an external devil, the jealous witch who hated Snow White; the other, the devil inside Snow White, who loved herself too dearly. First, the outside devil worked strictly on her own: "Have a nice apple, little girl? See how beautiful it is, how tasty it must be!" These temptations did not work. Snow White was a good person. She could not be tempted directly.

The animals and birds came to the rescue of their friend. They saw behind the ruse of the old hag, detected the evil, and spun the woman round and round until she was dizzy and breathless.

Then Snow White, kindness itself, showed exemplary compassion. She saw an opportunity to help a woman who needed her. She "did her good turn for the day" and offered her an arm to lean on, a chair to sit on, soup to gain strength by. Then the witch, the woman Snow White was helping, saw that she had her hooked. The outside devil worked on the inside devil:

My pretty thing, you have been so kind to me. You deserve a reward. The reward for being so kind is to have control over others. I have this apple, a magic apple. Take a bite and make a wish, and your wish has to come true. You will control the destiny—and the timing of your charming prince. He will be at the beck and call of your magic and you can force him to make you happy. After all, you deserve it. Have you not been good to the seven little people and most giving and charitable to me? Take a bite. You deserve to be rewarded.

Well, as you know, she bit (both literally and figuratively). But she was thwarted; destiny was not in her control. The prince did not show up. She was not rewarded.

So what did Snow White do then? She did what is typical for most good people: she went into a coma! (Now this "coma" can be drug addiction, alcoholism, an eating compulsion or gambling, or not speaking to people any more . . . or whatever despondent people devise in order to say no to life.) She was no longer any good for herself, or for the seven little people, or for anyone. Many days and weeks passed; Snow White gave up on everything, having no more opportunity to earn rewards, or to be in control of any giving-receiving relationship.

Of course, the happy ending ultimately did take place. But that happened outside of her control, so to speak. Snow White did not *make* happiness fall her way. She was powerless, "*coma*-ed," wallowing in her own pity-party because she had not been rewarded on schedule, "after all the good she did for others!"

It was Jesus Christ (aka Prince Charming) who took the initiative. In this story—and in everybody's story—it is always God (not we) who starts this business of love. Snow White's Prince came on *his* initiative and in *his* good time. He saw her need and he loved her well because she needed love. She was first loved, and then she loved back . . . and they still live, happily, ever after.

There's a bit of Snow White in us all. Most people are good

people who cannot be tempted in a straightforward way, by a straightforward devil. Not as a rule. If Satan were to suggest that we be directly selfish, or evil, or arrogant against our friends, these ruses usually would not work. So Satan becomes crafty: he "cons" us, using our goodness against ourselves.

The setup for the con job is: 1) faithfulness to duty (like Snow White cooking and cleaning the cottage), and 2) generous acts of kindness (like hospitality to the old hag). Then good people sit back and reflect:

> I am good, kind, faithful, generous in my giving relationships. It's time for me to be rewarded. The reward I want is control, magic control over the destiny of others: God to respond to my demands and on my time schedule, dreams of prosperity to come true, friends and family to be so grateful for my goodness to them they will do just what I want.

This was the mismanagement of the Pharisees in the time of Christ. The Pharisees were good people, upright, faithful, generous (according to their own scales). Their problem was that they harnessed merely human interpretations to the good they did. They assumed that initiative was theirs in all their actions; and even worse, they postured for privilege, based on the good they did, and presumed God's compliance to their demands.

Then Jesus came, preaching a different message: We do not take the initiative; God does. God begins the whole process of doing good. We simply receive this good and humbly do God's will, as a tenant farmer prospering on land that has been undeservedly bestowed. Jesus let the Pharisees know they were not in control of anything; his Father was. Theirs was only to be grateful for his initiating love.

Because Jesus said things like this, the Pharisees, good people that they were, contrived to have him crucified. Goodness without power was an insufferable situation for them. They defied our Lord with what was, for them, an unanswerable question: "What's the sense of doing good if I can't in some way control those I do good for?"

The Pharisees didn't like their role, and reacted outrageously. They rejected Jesus, even to the cross. That is one way to mismanage doing good works: complete rejection of the God (or friends) one cannot control.

The other way, Snow White's way, is the more favored procedure: fall into a coma, go to sleep on everybody (by way of drugs, drink, television addiction, hypochondria, silent treatment, etc.):

- People don't appreciate me for all the good I do for them!
- Nobody cares that I'm giving 80 percent to our marriage and only getting 20 percent back!
- That kid has 17 years worth of clothing and feeding and doctors' bills from me. All I ask him to do is fill out the image I have of him and get a haircut!
- I did them a favor once. It's time they did one for me!

On and on go the complaints. There is more righteous indignation and justified griping coming from the goodness of good people than from any other source. Perhaps this is why Jesus preferred the company of sinners to that of the righteous ones. He found it difficult to bear the noise of their well-documented grievances. At least sinners had the right disposition to receive the grace of God.

It is easy to do good to others, but it is not so easy to live with it afterward. There is a discipline of humility that is demanded and a delicate sensitivity to the pain of those on the receiving end.

St. Vincent de Paul saved many skid-row derelicts in Paris. Yet he would pray for hours and humbly ask his clients to forgive him for helping them. Kindness brings out a superior-inferior relationship—consoling for the giv*er*, but hard on the receiver.

When I help an old woman across the street, give a beggar a break, offer advice to a youngster, my giving points out the fact of their need. Unless they are extremely mature (or have quit on themselves entirely), they aren't going to like the inferior position my kindness reminded them of. Sometimes they will strike out against me, behaving defensively, for they resent my power acting on their relative powerlessness. At the very least, they will twist and turn in order not to be in my control. They may be grateful, but they will have their own ways of showing it, not mine.

There are no magic apples. Whenever good people expect rewards for their kindnesses, and become dejected when it doesn't happen, the goodness (which *was* goodness to begin with) turns sour in the soul. What starts as love changes into a manipulative ploy because of the afterthought desire to get something out of what was originally a gift.

The problem is not in the act itself. Most people are good in the first immediate instinct of their heart. The problem comes afterward, when soul sits back and says, "Okay, now it's my turn. What do I get back?" This is where humility must develop. The question is: "Was the giving act a good thing to do? Then let it be done. I'll not let the left hand of reflection know what the right hand of kindness so spontaneously took care of."

This is what Christ did. The 10 lepers (Luke 17:11–19) were cared for, even though only one returned to say thanks. Crowds were taught about the Eucharist (John 6:25-71), even though only a few were willing to believe. Christ cares, even though only a few care back.

This is what it means to be a Christian. All else is Pharisee-ism, mismanaged charity, and Snow White at her worst. We are to be like Christ: to do good because good is good to do, not because it gives us a bite of the magic apple of control.

8.

Managing Success

Sensitive to High Achievements

Suppose you are a marriage counselor. A friend of yours—a man we'll call Harry—meets you at the local diner. It's mid-afternoon and you are talking over a cup of coffee.

He gushes about a wonderful experience he just had. His company sent him to a five-day communication workshop. It was all about how to relate better with your fellow workers, family, and friends. It was a most impressive eye-opener. Harry was thrilled with new insights, new convictions, new techniques, and could not wait to tell his wife all about it . . . and the children . . . and to work out these newfound formulas with everyone on the job.

"Wow," he said, as he summed up his sensations. For the fifth time in the short ten minutes he said "Wow."

Would you warn him about his "Wows"? Would you suggest that, maybe, just maybe, if he insisted on recounting all the details of his exhilarating encounter, his family might get fed up with him . . . with it? Would you at least warn him about the possibility of some negative reactions to his bubbling exuberance?

If you would, then you are a good counselor. And your cautionary prudence would be very close to Christ's after he took Peter, James, and John for their "peak experience" on Mt. Tabor. They, too, had a "Wow" experience when they attended that marvelous communication workshop on the Meaning of the Messiah. The event is best described in St. Matthew's Gospel (17:1–2): "Jesus took Peter, James and his brother John and led them up on a high mountain by themselves. He was transfigured before their eyes. His face became as dazzling as the sun, his clothes as radiant as light."

What the disciples experienced was something truly marvelous. It was majestic, gratifying, consoling. They were, by association with Jesus, really "somebodies." No wonder Peter said, "Lord, it is good for us to be here!"

It wasn't much fun listening to Jesus when he promised them the cross or warned them they must let go of their own securities ("lose their life") if they wanted to find themselves in God. Our Lord's words six days earlier had saddened them. The challenge made them uncomfortable.

But this was exhilarating—it was a "wow." No wonder Peter said (Matthew 17:4–5), "'Lord, how good that we are here. With your permission I will erect three tents here, one for you, one for Moses and one for Elijah.' He was still speaking when suddenly a bright cloud overshadowed them. Out of the cloud came a voice which said, 'This is my beloved Son, on whom my favor rests. Listen to him.'"

The transforming experience of God's magnificent love made things clearer to the favored disciples; they saw how wonderful the Father is, and how much more enjoyable it would be to remain on the mountain than to go down below and return to the confusion of everyday life.

Jesus was gentle with them. He "came forward toward them and, laying his hands on them, said, 'Get up! Do not be afraid.'" But he did take them down from the "high" of the mountain and lead them back to the nitty-gritty waiting in the valleys and villages below. Love had to be proved by faithfulness; it could not simply be relished in the fond memory of weekend consolations.

Jesus warned them *not* to speak about what happened. They must wait until all the apostles had their own personal illumination after Easter (Matthew 17:9): "As they were coming down the mountainside, Jesus commanded them, 'Do not tell anyone of the vision until the Son of Man rises from the dead.'" You can imagine what would have happened if they went about blurting out their wonderful experience. No matter how sensitively they put it—and, at that time, neither Peter, James, or John were noted for their sensitivity to other people's feelings—it still would cause resentment in others.

Three of the Twelve enjoyed what nine of the Twelve had not. This automatically formed a have/have-not relationship. One-quarter of the group was "superior" to the others. Whenever such a thing happens, it is a very delicate situation. Most people—from arrogant pride or innocent enthusiasm—like to "lord it over" others by taking over the conversation and giving a triumphant recital of what wonderful things happened to them.

I heard a story once about three newly ordained priests who returned to their monastery after having made a special kind of retreat. The retreat was a moving thing for them—a "wow" experience. They reached a depth of understanding of the Lord and felt a joy in his presence in a way they never had before. They were enthusiastic and exuberant. But two of them had not yet left the mountain. One even said, in the company of 20 priests, "This is the first real retreat I ever made in my life!" Well, among that company of 20 priests were two who had given retreats to these same three men some years past. The sting of that proclamation was like a slap in the face for them. Worse than a slap in the face, it was a consignment to nonentity. It said, "You two priests did nothing for me. You are nobodies. The new experience was everything. It gave me all I have!"

That insult was not intended by the young priest. He was simply still on a high from what had happened and he paraded it. But that was how the words were interpreted by the "have-nots," especially by the two older priests who had hoped that the spirituality and the retreat conferences they had given were not altogether worthless.

One of the three young priests was more sensitive to the feelings of the "out group." He quietly expressed himself. He had the thoughtfulness—and good sense—to express himself in terms of a larger perspective. He related how the insights gained and the self-discipline acquired on previous retreats had helped him to be aware of the graces he had just received. He had the delicacy and tact to thank the two priests who had given him earlier retreats. He remembered links between the long past and the recent past. In this way, other people were included in his joy. They were drawn into his "have," not relegated to the category of "have-not."

There is a danger lurking in any "wow" experience. Without proper handling, something meant to be a gift of encouragement from God (a "consolation of the Spirit") can degenerate into vainglorious boasting or condescending triumphalism.

We are better than other people because:

- we made a Marriage Encounter.
- we made a 7-day directed retreat.
- we made a 30-day directed retreat.
- we have learned how to develop our intensive journal.
- we are experts in transcendental meditation.
- we are proficient in transpersonal awareness.
- we were on a beautiful workshop and learned all about prayer from Father ____, or all about healing from Guru ____.
- we are charismatic and have the gift of tongues and were baptized in the Spirit, not just in the ordinary baptism.

And so on. Add to this list other ways that people can have a peak experience—yoga, psychosynthesis, rich understanding drawn from a gifted teacher, a beautiful vacation somewhere, a deep-felt "wow" that came on a lonely beach when the sun was setting and the sea was calm, the smile of perfect trust from your own baby in your arms. The occasions are almost limitless. And no two people are alike.

These experiences, gifts from God, are not to be denied. They are reassurances, consolations, flashes of brilliant insight, spiritual adrenaline that keeps one going when the cross gets heavy. They are meant to be cherished and appreciated.

I am not suggesting that we abandon our visions or adventures, but only that we handle them with more emphasis on quiet gratitude to God for giving the experience rather than on robust backslapping ourselves for having received it. And I am most emphatically suggesting (in the spirit of Jesus cautioning his three disciples) that we be much more delicately sensitive to those who have not had the same experience in the same way. Any superior/inferior relationship brings out the worst in those who feel inferior. It makes them defensive.

There are two principal ways in which we can be superior. One way is by doing good for others, giving advice, money, care, help, support. It is easy to mismanage this kind of relationship. This is how Snow White got into trouble. The second way is to be superior by *experience*. Everyone knows how defensive youngsters can be when adults flaunt their superiority in this area:

- When I was your age, I walked to school—10 feet of snow, unlit streets, 20 pounds of books, cold classrooms. I had it tough!
- I've lived longer, and it's my car and my house and my money—so listen to me.
- I've learned by my experiences, and I want to spare you the hurts; so let me spoon-feed you my learning and never mind experiencing for yourself.

No wonder youngsters retaliate defensively. Nobody likes to remain in an inferior position. They think of ways to equalize the situation. Usually, it's in the area of emotions. They get their parents angry one way or another: sloppy clothes, messy hair, inattentiveness, raucous voice, picky appetite, etc. Then the adults get angry. This is a great equalizer. There is no longer a superior/inferior setting—all are equally irritated and irritable.

The same thing happens whenever anyone tactlessly displays newly found enthusiasm in the presence of others. A good experience is a "have," a cherished possession. It's important to remember that others are "have-nots" in regard to this experience. Demands of love impel the enthusiast to think of others, to include them in the joy of the experience (as they are able to be included), not to make them feel like second-rate, subhuman individuals.

I have pleaded with retreatants to be prudent about the way they return home and give an account of their weekend retreat. For most of the men and women who come to us, the weekend is very good. It constitutes a "wow" experience of sorts. Then the retreatants leave and meet their families on Sunday afternoon. What happens? So often their account of it is condescending.

- Honey, I wish you were there to hear what Father Markey said yesterday. It's something I've been trying to tell you for years!
- Kids, now I'm sure I'm right about what I've been trying to get through to you. I found out that Jesus agrees with me.

No wonder the rest of the family gets turned off! Wouldn't it be better to express yourself in a way that's sensitive to them? They have stayed home, without the car, eating chili and beans. You've been doing what they have had no part in. Bring them into your joy.

- Honey, I had a good weekend. I had a feeling of peace and love something like the feeling you had when you attended that workshop last year. And I thought of you often, how grateful I am for so many things you are for me. You were really with me.

•Kids, Father Markey said something to me that you've been trying to tell me for years. I see what you mean now. Thanks for telling me. Sorry it took so long to understand.

How can we show our love for those who were left behind? Jesus suggested to his three friends that they keep quiet until the other nine apostles, come Easter, will have seen the transformed Messiah with their own eyes. So one good idea is to be like Peter, James, and John and wait until your family and friends have had a wonderful weekend somewhat similar to yours. Another suggestion is to help them feel that they were a part of your newfound understanding all the time. This way, others will draw courage from the consolation God has given you, and Jesus will be praised for the many and varied options of divine exhuberance—as Jesus shows you flashes of his greatness . . . and then gently leads you back to your valleys and villages to get to work again.

9.

Two Shields
Against
Discouragement

Giving Jesus Easy Access

Please read aloud (and *over*dramatize) these two poems: "Folney Bird" and "Yes *But* Beasts." They describe a couple of moods that can severely restrict all kinds of communication, divine and human, sacred and secular. These are creatures that close things down. And the worst thing they do is to block Christ's gifts of love and prevent all chances for hope.

The first creature, "Folney," is pronounced with a long "o"; it's the contraction of "if only." Pretend you are alone, in your favorite sulking corner, with your face in its favorite pose of petulance. Then "ham it up" with these two poems to yourself:

The Folney is a funny bird
With noises like you never heard
And claws inside to tear its chest
And tears for eyes and gloom for guest.
It mopes about with broken wing
And has a monotone to sing,
The pity-pampered Folney Song:
"Folney . . ." "Folney . . ." all day long!
"Folney he . . ." or "Folney she . . ."
Or "Folney I, or they, or we . . ."
Or "Folney you were only there . . ."
Or "Folney you weren't so unfair!"
And on and on—the Folney Bird,
With sounds that sadness has inferred
And claws inside to tear its chest
And tears for eyes and gloom for guest,
It muffles feathers every day
And broken-wings its life away.

Its cousins are the Yes *But* Beasts
Wet-blanketing the joy of feasts,
Yes-butting into family hopes
And changing darlings into dopes.
They snarl when all the world would sing
And ruin almost everything.
"I want your help," they say at first;
"I like you," starts their song (rehearsed).
"You make good sense" (this phrase is nursed).
And then you must expect the worst:
"Yes, *but*," "Yes, *but* . . . I don't know . . ."
"I tried that once—it didn't go . . ."
"I have these reservations strong . . ."

"I know the reasons why you're wrong . . ."
"You have these faults . . ." "We have this lack . . ."
Who can resist against such flak!
One leaves the field defeated, daunted.
(That's what the Yes *But* Beasts had wanted.)
They leave to tear up other joys
And hope away from girls and boys
And pride away from men and Mses
And life into a failure's fizzes.
They want you in their same old rut;
They cannot bear nor song nor strut;
Their hope is shoo-ed, their heart is shut.
Beware of beasts that say, "Yes, but."

The Folney Bird and the Yes *But* Beast are still powerful devils and rule a great part of our world. Both attack the beautiful and innocent victim called *possibilities.* The Folney Bird attacks the rear; the Yes *But* Beasts devastate supply lines up front. One claws away at the past and hurts the memory; the other tears into the future and puts hope to rout.

The Folney Bird, broken-winging its life away, is that tendency of the heart to mope about with sad recitals of the past. It takes up possibilities that perhaps were valid at one time, but are not available any longer:

- A dentist: "If only I had decided to be a priest . . . had three boys instead of three girls . . . had been a truck driver with fewer worries . . . had moved to Chicago . . ."
- A priest: "If only I had decided to be a dentist . . . and had married . . . had three girls . . . had left Chicago . . ."
- A woman: "If only I had married Jim instead of Jack . . . or devoted a few more years to my career before I started my family . . ."

•Her husband: "If only I had studied more . . . or married later . . . or had a better football coach in high school . . . or taken that other job offer . . ."
•Her sister: "If only my parents were as rich as Rockefeller . . . or if only they had not talked me into staying here . . . or if only I were more attractive . . ."

And on and on.

Such litanies do no good. They stifle the present moment and the possibilities that are actually at hand. Often enough, too, they demoralize the people around us. Imagine how Jack feels when his wife sighs regretfully over her lost opportunity to marry Jim. (I remember that my dad always found some reason to leave the room whenever Mother would start talking about her old beaus and her lost chances.)

The present is the only period of time that has reality. The past no longer exists and the future hasn't come yet. All there is, is now. It is not good to go back over the past, pretending to have made other decisions, embraced a different destiny, made fewer mistakes or more money. The world we live in is the world we've come from—with all of its opportunities taken and opportunities rejected. The many hits and misses of our past have provided us with the present we live in. Let's get on with the job, learn from mistakes, be grateful for our successes, and attend to the possibilities that are current and actually controllable.

The other danger to possibilities is the Yes *But* Beast that deadens the future. The most obvious scars it inflicts are those celebrated by the introductory poem. "Yes, *but* . . ." is followed by some form of disclaimer: "It won't work!" or "I've already thought of that and discounted it."

Many novels and psychological books have analyzed the "rip-off" quality of the Yes *But* Beasts. There are two steps in this strategy. First comes the ploy: "I want advice." The other person gets hooked and offers some advice. Then comes the "rip-off": "Yes, but it won't work for these reasons . . ." The "game" consists in defeating the advisor, showing up the stupidity of the suggestion. Either that is the game, or else the person asking for advice is simply looking for sympathy, enlisting pity for a situation that has the doom of failure worked right into it.

The word "but" is a killer of possibilities and a killer of whatever statements preceded it. The word "and" is a conjunction. It joins. "But" is a dysfunction. It disavows, debilitates, and destroys.

Of course, sometimes it is necessary to use the word "but" (or *however* or *on the other hand*):

- I like you very much, *but* I'm married.
- It would be nice to drive a luxury car, *but* I just can't afford one.
- I'd like to join your organization; *however*, my family has prior claim on my time.

In such cases, "but" is a disciplinary word. When it is a choice of either/or, "but" must assert itself; options must be narrowed down to one. In many cases, though, "but" serves to effectively sunder what should be kept together:

- I like him, *but* he has some faults.
- She has a nice personality, *but* she's too pushy.
- He's a good worker, *but* I don't trust his drive.
- She's very intelligent, *but* she's probably stuck on herself.

Whenever we use "but" in a sentence, we really stand by whatever thought comes *after* the word; and we disavow, for all practical purposes, whatever went *before* it. A married couple came to me recently. They were talking about another couple. The man said, "They do get loud sometimes, *but* they're both a lot of fun to be with." The woman said, "They are a lot of fun at times; *but* I can't stand their boisterousness." In effect, he was saying, "Never mind their faults, I like them." She was saying, "Never mind their good qualities, I don't like them."

There's nothing wrong with this, as such. We do have preferences and priorities; and the way we normally express these is by expressing our real views in the clause that comes after "but." Very often, though, the word "and" can express our views with more honest presentation of the whole truth. "I like him, *but* he's too bold," really means: "There might be some likeable qualities about him but these are really unimportant. I really don't like him because he is too bold." "And" keeps it all together: "I like him *and* I dislike this quality in him. He's a mixed bag of good and bad, as we all are."

"And" has more balance to it; "but" only pretends to be balanced. There is an unspoken bias hiding behind the apparent fairness that seems to be taking up both sides.

Two priests were asked what they thought about the charismatic prayer movement. Both seemed to be balanced in their reply. One said, "Charismatics are impressive in some ways," which he listed; "*but* they seem dangerous and silly for these reasons," which he also listed. The other priest said, "Admittedly, there are some imprudent enthusiasts among them," and he went on to give an example. "*But* the love and joy so many of them manifest surely is a sign that God is with them."

It would be better for each to say: "This is the good *and* the bad of it; and for the reasons given, I take my stand for (or against)." This approach is more honest and responsible. The same could apply to any discussion of friends, politics, governmental decisions, or family differences. Use the word "and" to "let it all hang out." "But" dismisses too abruptly whatever statements came before it.

This is the most important part of the present chapter. Self-devastation is the worst of the bad-word world of "but." Who hasn't heard many variants of "I'm no good" statements coming out of this bad world? "Yes, I am kind to people, often helpful, popular with fellow workers, patient at times—*but* I'm impatient, too; *but* I'm selfish sometimes; *but* one of my bosses doesn't like me; *but* I'm not perfect."

So often "but" destroys the goodness that a person is and does, a hurt that is self-inflicted. Then, often enough, the hurt fans out. Jesus said, "Love others as you love yourself." This is, frequently, just what we actually do; we can't stand ourselves (because we've been concentrating on the bad side of ourselves), so we treat others the same way. We start out with the statement: "I have some good qualities, *but* they don't count because of these flaws." Then we treat others the same way: "They might have some good qualities, *but* they aren't perfect either." So they are relegated to the "no good" conclusion, too!

The way to self-healing (and from self-healing, other-people-healing) is to keep together the whole mix of good and bad. Replace "but" with "and": "I am patient *and* impatient, kind *and* selfish, joyful *and* depressed, liked *and* disliked,"etc.

This way, we will be rescued from the demoralizing process that concludes with an "I'm no good" attitude because all is not perfect. We will learn to appreciate better, and to develop more confidently, the good side of our personality.

One advantage of the "I am both good *and* bad" attitude is that we have a better place from which to work. Possibilities for self-improvement open up. We can, without panic or depression, take a good look at the selfish side of our behavior and do something about it. We can understand that some unhappy situations are caused by circumstances outside our control. We can then develop ways of coping with them, which is better than wringing our hands, spending unhappy hours in the fruitless wish that "they" would change.

Because it's no longer an either/or question ("I am either perfect or I'm no good at all"), we can calmly investigate what the elements are that change us from behaving well to behaving sinfully, and what the qualities are that change us back again from bad to good. Then we can manage our lives with more control, asking the less dramatic, more workable question: "How can I improve myself and help others, little by little?"

Another way of using the healing word "and" is in the area of other people's approval or disapproval. The bad-word world of "but" demands 100 percent:

- I get along with most of my co-workers; *but* Charlie can't stand me, so is it any wonder that I'm unhappy all the time?
- My spouse and I are doing fine most of the time; *but* he (she) criticizes me about this one thing. Once a week we quarrel. So what's wrong with our marriage?

The joining word "and" interprets these situations with a more conciliatory and inclusive attitude. It delivers us from death-dealing discouragement:

- Well, if nine co-workers like me and Charlie despises me, that doesn't mean I'm no good. Nine out of 10 is a good average. I'll accept dislike from some and won't let it keep me away from the joy of the friends I have.

•One day out of seven means that on six of seven days my spouse and I are doing fine. Eighty-five percent is a good average. Maybe the good days can help us heal the bad ones. I'll not deny the happiness we have just because there's still room for improvement in both of us.

The healing ways of "and" is another aspect of Christ's "sun and rain" commandment of love. God the Father does not hurl the word "but" at people. ("I'll send you my sun and rain if you are good, *but* not if you are bad!")

God gives sun and rain to honest *and* dishonest people— *both*! And so must we. Furthermore, God sends us "sun and rain" on our own good side and bad side, on our good days and bad days. The patient Love of God is ready to be applied by Jesus Christ himself. He will make his positive contributions. Our work is to prepare for his comings by reducing the negatives. Once we have caged the Folney Bird and have muzzled the Yes *But* Beasts, we'll be in good shape. The door will be open and the welcome mat will be right there waiting . . . and the virtue of hope will introduce us to the graciousness of God.

10.

Sometimes
Simplicity
Doesn't Work

Healthy Complexity

Many years ago at our Passionist Monastery in Boston, I was one of 12 seminarians studying St. Paul's Letter to the Romans. During a period of recreation, we had a long and heated discussion, still warm from the interesting class lecture. Brother Cook was with us, and he was bored. He didn't *say* he was bored. He said, "Look, friends, will you please tell me, in a nice simple sentence—without any adornments or phrases that keep going on and on—just *what* St. Paul was talking about?" We replied, "Yes, we'll do this if you will tell us, in one simple sentence—without any detailed elaborations—just what your responsibilities are as the cook here." He said, "I can't do it in a sentence. I've got to order, arrange diets, meet with sales reps, check for bargains, plan menus, etc." We then responded, "If you won't grant us the complicated nature of what we love, we won't allow for the complexities of what you love."

This story dramatizes one of the dangers of simplification. Sometimes things should become more simple; at other times they should stay complex, where they belong.

Our last half-century has seen a lot of pressure put upon communicators to KISS (Keep It Simple, Stupid!). Since the computer invasion, it has become even more necessary that all message makers guarantee that they are "user friendly."

Good point. In many situations, simplicity takes high priority. Indeed, I decided to write this book because I march under the banner of KISS. I wanted to talk about certain attitudes and certain necessary conditions for growth the way friends talk about things around their kitchen tables. I don't like the word "stupid" applied anywhere, to anyone. But I do take the other words to heart: serious matters should be discussed in a language that is least likely to be tiresome or misunderstood.

This is one stand I firmly take, upon *one* foot. Only one; not two, because the KISS approach is good only in certain respects. There is another banner I wave, also: KICK (Keep It Complicated, Kid!) I take my stand under this slogan even more emphatically. Of course, one is directly opposed to the other. But, while a KISS is a good way to relate information, we would do well to put up with KICK in the areas of friendship, philosophy, and religion.

Jesus said (Matthew 6:21): "Where your treasure is, there your heart is also." It could be paraphrased: "Wherever your interest is, there you will be patient with complexity." Brother Cook was not interested in St. Paul's theology. He wanted to get away from this subject ("Keep it simple!"). He was avidly interested in his work, and knew the importance of it, and so he was appreciative of, even fascinated by, its varied demands and rich complexity.

I know of a married couple who loved each other well—*except* for two areas of complexity. Area 1: The husband was not handy around the house. The lawn, for instance, could go unnoticed for weeks. He was an excellent basketball coach. So, predictably enough, he was an advocate of "keep it simple" when it came to the home; yet he was a patient perfectionist on the court, rich with knowledge about four corners, fast breaks, pivot plays, second and third options, and a thousand more minute realities that gave him winning teams. He could spend hours developing the flow of one youngster's foul shooting style; he found it difficult to spend half an hour cutting grass.

Area 2: The wife kept the home running smoothly. She was patient with details, capable of balancing all the many-faceted demands of domesticity, a competent juggler of tasty meals, bills, transportation for the kids, school responsibilities, laundry, water leaks, discount sales, etc. She loved it all. Because she loved it, she was an able "complexionist" in this area. But she cared little for sports. She tended to "keep it simple" as far as her husband's job was concerned: "My husband? Oh, he goes to school and throws out a basketball and lets the boys play; and he never gets home until late and he's away a lot because he has to go on trips."

Very often, a KISS is really a kiss-off. It's a common way for one person to say, "I really don't care!" to another:

• A farmer's life? Simple. Just get up, milk the cows, get the eggs, and wait for the sun and rain to grow the vegetables.
• A doctor? Simple. Take the pulse, write illegible prescriptions, and overcharge the patients.

• A housekeeper? Get up, make the breakfast, send everybody off on time, prepare the supper, and spend the rest of the day watching soap operas on TV. Simple!

• A parish priest? Nothing to do all week but say Mass in the morning. Simple!

The world we love is always complicated. Listen to any conversation among nurses, farmers, mechanics, mothers, bishops, plumbers, secretaries, even children playing cops and robbers. We can marvel at the rich variety of things to think about, talk about, and keep in touch with.

If strangers dare to simplify those areas of life we are really interested in, they will be laughed at or despised: "They just don't understand!" Simplification usually amounts to amputation:

• Trees are nothing but stuff for lumber. So cut down all the trees and leave a desert of stumps where there once was a lovely forest. Simple.

• A human being is just a thinking machine. So let's live as though emotions don't exist. Simple.

• Politicians (or priests or mothers or TV repair persons) are evil sometimes. Therefore don't trust any of them. Simple.

We get into trouble by working out of a KISS/kiss-off procedure in religion, too. It seems inconsistent that normally adult people want their religion simple: "Just tell me what I can and can't do, and what I can get away with so I don't go to hell, and keep the language in a style that a six-year-old can understand . . . and don't make it complicated!"

Yet, the same people demanding such childish simplicity from their religion:

- know almost enough medical terminology to pass a doctor's exam;
- know the intricate requirements of cosmetics well enough
  to work for a beauty parlor;
- have such a patient appreciation of spark plugs, trans-
  missions, batteries, and whatnot they could build their
  own automobile;
- delight so in the manifold maneuvers of pro football
  (flanker pass, blind-side block, mousetrap play, etc.) it
  could make one's head swim.

What is to be concluded from all this? That physical health
is intricately more important than spiritual health, beauty is
more interesting than goodness, cars mean more than God, the
patterns of football are more lively than the words of Jesus
Christ.

Isn't this the story of every heresy? In the interest of keeping
it simple, heresy amputates the complex nature of God's revelation. Jesus, for instance, is both God *and* man. "That's too
complicated," say the heretics. "Let's simplify theology to make
God easier to work with. Let's say Jesus was God and he was
only 'play acting' as a man, just pretending." Or: "Let's say
that he was only a man—one of the best men who ever lived,
granted—but only a man. Then we can cut him down to our
size and we don't have to take so seriously his command to
follow him. We will think of him as our 'brother,' not as our
Lord."

God is both merciful *and* just. "This is too complicated," say
the heretics. Then they choose again. Some say, "Let's simplify
and make God all justice; then, if anybody sins, he'll go to hell
without a second chance." Others say, "Let's simplify and
make God all kindness, so there is no hell; we can do anything
we want and then 'get around' God as we used to get around

Santa Claus when we were kids."

God is the source of life and health and healing; he is also the giver of brains to people like doctors who learn how to cure sickness. Heretics who concentrate on the first statement say, "That's too complicated! Let's keep it simple by giving God, and *only* God, the right to heal. Therefore we must avoid doctors as the work of the devil."

Other heretics, like some secular materialists, say "Miracles are impossible. God has no power to intervene or heal; only doctors and gurus can do such things!" Simple.

The Catholic church keeps it complicated. We agree with those who defend God's power to heal in the *positive* statements they make. We have Lourdes; we pray, just before Holy Communion, "Lord, say only the word and I shall be healed." And we also reverence the healing power of medical science.

In all the disagreements with heretics, we do not dispute what they affirm. We dispute what they deny, what they leave out. We hold on to the complicated nature of our faith, even though we are faced with mystery by doing so: God is one *and* three at the same time; humans are predestined by God *and* given a responsible free will at the same time; Jesus is God *and* man at the same time; the Lord demands that we be "guileless as doves *and* as shrewd as a snake" at the same time.

It is tempting, in these and other aspects of our faith, to make it simple. Things are easier to deal with and more congenial to a flabby spirit and a lazy mind. In those areas of life we don't really care about, we want things as easy as possible. But we can't do this in the area of our faith, which registers our degree of friendship with God. In this area, "Keep it complicated, kid!"

Jesus knows when he is treated with interest and when he is given the kiss-off of simplification. He wants us to puzzle over his paradoxes and parables (Mark 4:33–34):

By means of parables
he taught the people
in such a way that they could understand.
[But] to them he spoke *only* by way of parables,
while he kept explaining [their meaning]
privately, to his disciples. (Italics added)

Jesus wanted them—and us—to grope for further meaning
of his messages. We are warned not to dismiss him as "just another storyteller" who spoke parables to the people in order to
keep it simple.

The disciples grew into understanding, keeping in touch
with all the complexities of their baffling faith. And so must
we. We must be as sensitive to the manifold movements of
God's grace as a mother is to the varied moods and purrs and
danger signals of her infant. We must be as patient with complexity as a coach planning strategy for his ball team, as a
brother preparing meals in a monastery, as a hypochondriac
reading up on all the latest medical discoveries.

We must be like Mary. She did not fully understand her role
or the complex nature of her son's mission. Nevertheless, she
did not stunt herself with impatient demands that her Son, to
take one example, "keep it simple" when she and Joseph
found their 12-year-old son who had been lost for three days.
Mary was mystified both by her Son's behavior and by his response, but she didn't try to understand things too quickly.
She was a competent "complexionist," someone who proved
worthy of the Father's trust (Luke 2:51; see also 2:19, 1:29):

Mary kept all these things carefully,
treasuring them,
pondering them over and over in her heart.

11.

Helping Your Feelings Along

Three Turns in the Healing Process

Take the case of Norman, an insurance man. At work, he is confident about himself and enjoys the esteem of his fellow workers. He is proud of the good service he gives his clients; he trusts his instincts on the job. Chances are, he will do the right thing and give them the right advice. Wonderful.

But he is not this loving to his family. Perhaps he is fearful about his children's reputation, anxious about their present imperfections, resentful at times of their stubbornness. He doesn't trust his instincts in this area. He hasn't really loved his family enough. He may be clutching them possessively and *calling* it love, but possessiveness is not love. He must go against his instincts, which would in this case be to nag his children. He must love because he has to; he is not yet free to "love and do as he will."

Indeed, most people can trust their instincts with people outside their homes. The sense of appreciation for others and alertness to be of service to them is usually quite important. Yet most cannot trust their natural inclinations with their own family. Possessiveness, anxiety, the unwillingness to forget past hurts—these are often the predominant forces in a family, precisely the forces that obstruct true love.

Also, and especially, we cannot trust ourselves with ourselves. As a rule we love ourselves least of all. The instincts of depression, self-pity, anger, rancor, and the like are heavy in the heart. We cannot obey our quick impulses the way we can when we advise a friend we love unpossessively. We must love ourselves even when we don't care to. Also, when we have wronged someone, we must make amends, learn by the mistake, and keep going, even when we don't want to do this, either.

This is one way to grow. If we change our behavior patterns, we will be able to change the way we *think* about life and *feel* about it. We may not understand why we should love ourselves and our family; we may not always agree that it is reasonable to do so, in this or that case, but: "Jesus says we have to, so we have to!" Then, once the habit of good deeds develops, our minds will gradually come to the conclusion that the kind of behavior that nourishes and supports others is more pleasant and more productive than critical behavior that is constantly on other people's backs. Finally, when our thinking in this regard improves, all those feelings of the heart will change to an *up*beat. We will love ourselves more, be more sensitive to others, and have a heart-sure confidence in God's goodness, too.

In short: first, we do the works of love; then we think about how proper this is; finally, our hearts rejoice, our hurts relent, our anxieties relax . . . and soon it becomes second nature for us to live like Christ: authentically.

That is the first turn of the healing process: the outside level, or the beginners' circle, in changing attitudes and healing hurts. We behave in loving ways . . . and so improve the style of thinking about all the important stuff of life . . . and both these will put to bed those hateful movements of the heart and the worrisome naggings in the head . . . and we'll feel better.

Another way to start the process is to begin with the second turn of what might be called "wellness interactions." This second aspect is what we normally call education; it's the ordinary way schools operate. The idea is to generate the brainpower. Give a person more time to think about it and he will grow. He will have more reasons to behave in the right way because he has the means to think them through. His imagination will be stimulated and good feelings about himself will increase. Confidently and naturally, he will mature.

This, too, is a good method. Jesus certainly brought us to his school and taught us our lessons. Most of his parables were generators of thought. The Kingdom of God is like a farmer; a fisherman; a woman finding a lost coin; a father of a prodigal son; a mother hen with her chicks; a man preparing a wedding feast; a woman giving birth; a supplier of sun and rain; a giver of bread, not stones. Thanks to him, we have many beautiful ways of thinking about God and grace, which influence our behavior. This gives us new ways of feeling about God and ourselves; it stirs our imagination and we grow.

The third way—the one closest to our innermost self—is also a good method of education. It is different from the behavior processing from the outside layer ("Do it, or else you won't get the reward"). It is also different from the thought processing of the middle layer ("Do it to get more brainpower"). This one says, "You can do it. It's worth doing. You are worthwhile doing it."

This works on processing the feelings. If the feelings are healthy:

- thoughts can come easily to mind;
- imagination can be quickly stirred to pull thoughts together in fascinating arrangements;
- energy coming from this source can supply new thoughts with hopeful possibilities;
- good conduct and virtuous deeds can snap into action almost instinctively (like a good ballplayer performing intricate moves with ease because he feels good about his own ability and trusts the competence of his teammates).

But if the feelings are not healthy, then thinking is blocked, the heart is frozen with anxiety, and behavior is afflicted with a choice (or combination) of boredom, depression, frustration, disdain, or ruthless determination to get even.

It would seem obvious, therefore, that the first step of any educational system is to heal unhealthy feelings. No sense in sending a child off to school to learn how to think if anxieties tell her she can't learn, or if depression tells her there's nothing worthwhile to be gained from it. No sense in telling her to behave herself if boredom has a hold of her, telling her, "What's the difference, anyway?"

First comes healing. It must, if the feelings inside the heart are sick. This is the most basic, and favorite, style of education Jesus used. He always healed before he taught. Most frequently, he healed by expelling the devil from people who were possessed. (For "possessed by the devil" understand "possessed by the spirit of depression, self-pity, bitter resentments, the will to die rather than the will to live.")

Whether people were blind, lame, deaf or, especially, possessed, Jesus healed them first. Then, once they felt good about themselves and were "put together better," he taught them about the Kingdom of his Father. Finally, with these two experiences of support, he finished his teaching on the level of behavior: "If you love me, conduct yourselves in obedience to the commandment of love that you have seen in me. If you do, my Father will reward you with everlasting life."

Jesus concentrated on the inner layer. He repeated and repeated:

- It is I. Do not be afraid! (Matthew 14:27)
- Why are you so terrified? Why are you so lacking in faith? (Mark 4:40)
- Do not let yourselves be troubled (John 14:1).
- Do not let your hearts be troubled, or be afraid (John 14:27).
- These things I have spoken to you so that you may not be scandalized (fearful, demoralized) (John 16:1).

Over and over and over, Jesus healed people's feelings. Fears took priority. He ministered to them first, assuaging their twofold fear of *being unloved* (left out of friendships, rejected by significant people, not listened to, not cared about, unlovable) and *being ineffective* (discouraged by lack of attainment, put down for imperfect achievement, ridiculed for inept efforts, not considered a good child, youth, parent, worker, thinker).

If this was Jesus' method, it should be ours as well. The other two methods of helping people are good and should be used, knowing right and wrong and the difference between acceptable and unacceptable behavior. We learn them by doing them, learning as we go along, growing from the experiences.

We must also go to school. Unless we are helped to think for ourselves, we are only a kitchen robot or a couch potato. We cannot grow if we don't have the tools to think for ourselves.

But most important is the art of healing as Jesus practiced it. One of the most outstanding examples happened on Easter Sunday when Jesus met his disciples for the first time since he died. They were discouraged about themselves, unmanned by fear, hurting with the guilt of having played the coward.

Jesus forgave them, concentrating on their feelings. Then he spoke those healing words: "As the Father has sent me, so I send you" (John 20:21). The meaning was: "Go ahead; you can do it. Be the leaders of my church. I trust you."

Jesus did not bawl them out or reprimand them for their errant behavior, didn't lecture them as students who had just flunked. He healed them of their depression and anxieties and gave them confidence again. He showed he was counting on them, despite their imperfections. They moved on from there, becoming great saints and the pillars of the church. Their feelings were healed, so all three layers of their hearts were whole again.

Everyone is invited to this same time-of-goodness the apostles enjoyed. Jesus calls us to be freed from unhealthy fears, relieved of oppressive anxieties, delivered up from the possessiveness of sadness. When the change comes, we will have ears more open to teaching, and wills more eager to be trained in the love-style of our Lord. Then God's plan for a happy ending for us will shape up. The three parts of our personality—behaving, thinking, feeling—are turning together in the same twist. Things are working out a little better than they used to. And we continue to trust the last words Jesus said as he rejoined his Father in that place where he has made room for us. "Remember," he told us, "I am with you always . . . all ways."

12.

Forgiving
Yourself

". . . this day with me in Paradise"

This chapter on self-forgiveness is addressed to you, Mr. and Mrs. F.F. Americus, and the millions like you who sometimes sign their names with the initials "F.F."—fear of failure.

There are so many of you and an especially high percentage of parents, grandparents, teachers, clergy, and other well-meaning people who have good hearts, high hopes for certain people . . . and, at times, a bad track record about the outcome of the very ones they tried so hard to help.

At times of apparent failure, you begin by asking, "Where did I go wrong?" "What did we do wrong?" "What went wrong?" "Why didn't we realize sooner that . . . ?" "Why won't she talk to me any more?" Such questions, sometimes asked to the bathroom mirror, are invariably accompanied by worried eyes and a sad, defeated face. The detailed accounts may vary, but the puzzlement and self-inflicted hurt remain the same. "We don't know what went wrong," wonder the parents of a wayward son. "We brought him up right. He went to church with us every week. We sent him to learn his catechism. We sacrificed so he could go to a Catholic school. We gave him our love and our values."

Then comes the final part of the story that spells out failure: "But he doesn't go to church any more. He scorns our faith. He's taking dope and is into crime. He ran away from home and never sees us. He doesn't care about himself at all." And the clincher: "He turned out to be no good."

Many people will even quote our Lord's words in a fearful whisper as they dig deeper into the doom of guilt (Matthew 7:17): "Jesus told us that sound trees bear good fruit; but a bad tree bears bad fruit! I have borne a child that turned out bad. Therefore, I must be bad. I have failed God!" Of course, this is a most misleading and incorrect interpretation of Jesus' words. He was not speaking of parents who bring children to birth. He was speaking of each individual's free will and awesome responsibility to either do good or do evil. The things we do and the words we say are the particular assessment of who we are. "By their deeds you will know what's inside them!"

Still, even with the right understanding of Scripture, the hurt won't go away. There is a fine line between taking proper responsibility for bringing up children and taking on so much responsibility that it hurts. Many people go too far and drape the cloak of misery over themselves for developments that were not in their control.

How do I respond to those who grieve because they seem to have failed someone under their care? Here is what I sometimes say to them:

You say you taught them your faith and sent them to religion classes and even to Catholic schools. That doesn't
make things automatic. I know a man who was tutored in
religion for three years with the best educator of
Christian doctrine who ever lived. Tutored! He didn't just
have a class on Friday afternoon. That's all he took—
religion. And yet he learned so little from it all—so very
little—that he betrayed his teacher for 30 pieces of silver.

Are we to say that Jesus is a "bad tree" because Judas
turned out to be "bad fruit"? Preposterous! All 12 apostles received the same teaching and training. Some got it; some
didn't. Jesus was hurt by Judas's failure, but he wasn't crushed
by the hurt. He didn't neglect to love the others who were developing under his tutelage.

He didn't. But many good people do.

I have this dream about the parents of the good thief.
Nobody knows their names; we don't even know their son's
name. Tradition calls the good thief St. Dismas (Greek for
"right") because he was crucified on the cross that was to the
right of Jesus. So let's call his parents Mr. and Mrs. Dismas. In
my dream they had nine other children, who were more or less
neglected. Mom and Dad weren't thinking much about them;
they focused their tormented minds upon the unalterable past
that had turned one son into what they considered a failure.
Goaded by guilt, they asked themselves over and over:

What went wrong? Won't God punish us for the way our
son turned out? How can we hold our heads up in pub-
lic? What was the mistake we made? We sent him to the
synagogue. We taught him right from wrong. We tried to
do our best. How did we fail?

For years and years they wrung their hands and worried themselves sick and let all their energy just drain away. And what about the other nine children in their family? They were relegated to a kind of limbo. It wasn't that their parents disliked them. No. It's just that all their parents' love and reasons for living were spent on the one child who didn't care anyway! Nine children could have grown up better if their parents had shown them a happier outlook on life and a healthier self-confidence. They were shortchanged because their Mom and Dad decided (without giving God a chance to speak), "We're no good, because our son Dismas turned out no good!"

So many years of pointless misery! That is how it turned out in their case. They had foredoomed their son a failure. But he wasn't. He was blessed by Jesus himself—the only person, on record, who was canonized before he died. Jesus told him on Good Friday afternoon (Luke 23:43) "This day, you will be with me in Paradise." He is the good thief, a certain saint. But it is only for the last afternoon of his life that we call him good.

I don't know how Mr. and Mrs. Dismas accepted their parental implications or how they managed all those years when their son was considered a "no-good thief." I'm not certain that they made themselves as miserable as I imagine them doing. I only know that many, many parents have reacted this way, and I projected their stories on to the parents of the Good Thief.

This scene of "made-up Scripture" should encourage all those many people of different walks of life who focus their tormented minds upon their failures. I plead with them:

Don't worry, all of you Mr. and Mrs. Dismases of the world! You've done what you could. You tried. Don't judge anybody as "no good"—that last afternoon hasn't come yet. Keep communication lines open, pray for the final outcome of your "good thief," and go back and put your energies into caring for the people with you now. Don't neglect your spouse or family or friends, grieving over the loss of someone who is not there. Don't make them feel unable to make you happy. Let them begin again to look forward to a joyful home, an interesting talk, a gracious presence. Leave the lost one to the Lord, and to your prayers, and to his last afternoon.

It sometimes happens in many families and often in the lives of the saints that a good woman and a bad woman come from the same upbringing; they may even be twin sisters. Or a family from Manhattan's east side boasts a good priest-son but are shamed by a gangster-son.

So it was with Mr. and Mrs. Borromeo. Among their 20 children, they had twin sons, Charles and Anthony, who had the same dinner table, the same baptism, teaching, books, environment, play, punishment, the same Jesus in Holy Communion, and the same opportunities to be good or bad.

Charles Borromeo turned out to be a saint, a learned bishop, a writer of books, an altogether good man, "devoting all his household goods to provide for the needy, visiting the plague-stricken constantly, consoling them in a wonderful way" (Roman Breviary, November 8). Tony, his twin, turned out to be what we would call today the head of a crime family in northern Italy. He was an altogether unsavory character—the rackets, murder for hire, white slavery, the works.

What were Mr. and Mrs. Borromeo to say? If they were to brag, "Look, neighbors, look at our son the bishop, our son the saint, our son the hero. See how well we brought him up," their neighbors would respond, "Get off your pedestal, Mr.

and Mrs. Borromeo. Look at Tony, his twin brother. He turned out to be an evil good-for-nothing!"

Nor could the parents wring their hands, as Mr. and Mrs. Dismas did: "What did we do wrong? Look at what happened to Anthony. After all we tried to do—sent him to the best schools, even! God must be ashamed of us. How can a good tree bear bad fruit?" I must respond:

Don't be saddened, Mr. and Mrs. Borromeo. Look at Charles. You did the same for him. Rejoice in this. One out of two is not bad. Now go back to the other children who need your love and generous support. Each person must go through his own mystery of grace and responsiveness to grace. All parents can do is be present to each as much as possible, let time and the pace of God's love work with individual free will, and determine to worry only about things that are in their control.

I have concentrated on parents in this chapter, the Mr. and Mrs. Dismases and the Mr. and Mrs. Borromeos of the world. Their sense of failure is the most poignant; they need healing most of all. Even so, the same considerations apply to anyone in the helping professions—teachers with students, priests with penitents, social workers with clients, trainers with recruits, caregivers with their patients. This applies, also, to a friend who has lost a friend. In any of these situations, there can be mourning over the failure to reach a student, to help a client, to be a friend to someone who is now a friend no longer.

There are four ways of looking at past failures, four different concluding statements to pin on lost responsibility:

•The failure was mostly your fault.

•The failure was partly your fault, partly the other person's
  fault.
•The failure was mostly the other person's fault.
•There was no fault on either side—it's just the way things
  worked out.

The first two cases—failures due to real faults in *you*—need
a chapter of their own, the one coming up. Go to confession,
learn by past mistakes, have compassion on others who make
mistakes (you aren't perfect either, remember), and keep going
with the healing grace of God.

In the fourth case—the "no-fault" failure—the best thing to
do is leave it alone. Here is an example of what I mean by a no-
fault hurt: One day on her way home from school, a little girl
bent down to pick two or three beautiful spring flowers. As
she did so, her school books slipped from her arms and landed
in a puddle. She paid no attention to the muddy books; all her
interest was on the flowers, picked for her mother to enjoy.
She met her mother on the front porch and said, "Here,
Mommy. Aren't they beautiful?" Her mother couldn't see the
flowers, but only what her daughter didn't notice. "Look at
those books! Don't you care how much we sacrifice so you can
go to school? Don't you care at all?"

Mother and daughter loved each other. They simply had
two different sets of values and they failed to understand the
love that was expressed so differently. Just because a failure is
no-fault doesn't mean it doesn't hurt. It hurts as much—
perhaps more—than any other kind. The point is that it's use-
less to fret over no-fault failures as though they were blame-
worthy. If, as in this case, it is a failure of perception on both
sides, we can help to widen the perceptions. We can't help by
berating the perceivers.

The third case is what I touched on in this chapter. You tried to help, or teach, or coach, or train, or bring your kids up right. Some of your efforts didn't "take." You failed through no fault (no serious or deliberate fault) of your own. Well, there are other children in your family who need a living Mom and Dad, not two half-alive parents who have dug their own graves prematurely.

Jesus told his disciples (Luke 9:5–6) to "Shake the dust from your feet (as you leave those people who refuse to listen to you). This will bear witness that you tried, but they resisted you. Then go to another town." That is what they did. They didn't sit on the roadside and groan with misery because some people wouldn't accept them. There were plenty of other places to go, plenty of other people who *would* receive them. "And they set out and went from village to village, spreading the good news everywhere and curing diseases."

The meaning is clear: it's not good to wear yourself out with self-recriminations. And anyway, who says "failure" is really a failure? Because the crowd in Jerusalem demanded that Jesus be crucified—a fact that shows that our Lord did not win everyone over—does this indicate that Jesus was a failure? Only God can judge who is, and who is not, a failure.

And God has strange ways of reevaluating Mr. and Mrs. Dismas's little boy. A bad thief turned out to be the good St. Dismas. It seems right to add one phrase to the last words Jesus spoke: "This day, you *and your parents* will be with me in Paradise."

If you know people who are eating their hearts out over something they cannot control, tell them the story of St. Dismas and St. Charles Borromeo and perhaps some of the happy endings you personally know about. Tell them, "Who knows how things will end? The last afternoon hasn't come yet."

13.

The Gift of Peace

A Booster Shot of Love

Suppose you know a non-Catholic woman who agrees with many teachings of Catholicism, but the idea of confessing to a priest is repugnant to her. She says, "Why tell my sins to a priest? I'll go directly to God and express my sorrow. Jesus already knows all about my wrongdoings. Even so, he understands my basic goodness and he forgives me."

Suppose too that you know a non-practicing Catholic man who goes to church sporadically; he's a "Social Christian." Most aspects of the faith he still believes in, but he would never go to confession because of his concern about personal authenticity. "Why be a phony?" he says. "I'll only go right back and do it again!"

How would you respond to these two individuals and their

honest problems with this sacrament? What would you say to each? How would you say it? How do you suppose Jesus would respond to them? What would he say, and what would his manner be? Finally, put yourself into the mind and heart of Saint Peter, Easter Sunday afternoon, when he and his associates had been given the Sacrament of Pardon and Peace for the very first time. What would St. Peter say to this man and woman? There may be different responses for the three instances.

To elaborate more fully, let us think about how Jesus might talk about the sacrament. Perhaps it would be best to approach Christ's attitude indirectly, in ordinary human terms. Say you have a friend who hurt your feelings somehow, or insulted or betrayed you. He has denied your friendship. When he realized what he had done, he was sorry. But he never came to tell you that himself. You heard about it from others. You *know* he is sorry, *he* knows he is sorry, but there is something still missing. You wish he would come to you and shake hands so that you could tell him, "That's okay. Glad we're friends again. Let's forget what happened and start again." Unless he lets you forgive him, there is still something missing in your heart.

So it is with Jesus. There are things he wants to say to us and do for us. He wants to tell us on a one-to-one basis, friend-to-friend, into our eardrums, so that we can't miss it and be confused by worries, fears, and guilt bouncing around in our mind:

I'm glad you're here. Now I can tell you—out loud—that I love you. I forgive you and I want you to forgive yourself. I want you to be free from your sadness about your weakness. It's hard enough living in the present without . brooding about the past and wasting energy with enervating self-reproach or bitterness or guilt. I love you now. Come on, let's shake hands, and let's make friendship grow from here.

Our instinct about God is that he is a *celebrator*—not only the *source* of love and life, but the communicator and celebrator of them, too. Forgiveness is, supremely, an act of love. Indirectly, it is a link to life—more life, fuller life, growing from the fresh handshake. The handshake has to take place, and it has to do so with appropriate ceremony. It's no good to be sneaky or one-sided, leaving the merciful God in the dark, not permitting God to see our sorrow, celebrate the divine mercy, or enjoy this most delightful act of love—forgiving.

How fortunate that we now can go to confession in a way that is more personal than the way we used to go. We give more time to God's responsiveness. We emphasize the active pleasure of reconciliation with God, rather than our work of wading through past sins. Now we can better understand that Jesus' mercy is primarily a cause for celebration. It is experienced in an open manner, rather than performed in a place suggestive of shadows, muffled whispers, and secrecy—things more associated with crime in the dead of night than with a display of love given by a God who sent the Son precisely to make this moment possible.

Let us observe Christ at perhaps the most dramatic event that showed the dynamism and delight of his forgiving love. To find out what to look for, we put ourselves into the personality of a man who was so much like us, with all our good and bad, our noble side and ignoble side. The man was Simon Peter. His documented story covers three years, from his first call in Galilee to his lonely sorrow on the evening of Good Friday, to the forgiveness of Easter. A good man and a strong leader, Peter had natural talents in abundance and an obvious love for Jesus that made him special. But he had his faults. He was overconfident of his strength, pushy with his ideas, and impatient with people he felt were wasting the Master's time.

And then he fell. He sinned. It was the kind of sin most of us commit; the desire for human respect caused him to deny the kind of person he really was. Around the bonfire, near the court of the high priest, soldiers and serving girls were goading him and making fun of him for his Galilean twang and his attachment to a disgraced nobody. He caved in to this gang pressure and denied his love for Jesus.

When he realized the implications of his weakness, he felt very bad and wept bitterly. No doubt he told God how sorry he was, as he cried all by himself, all night long.

But still there was something missing. Look where Simon Peter was on Easter Sunday—behind doors that were locked because of fear. The fear was there, even though he already was contrite in his heart. He was afraid of more than reprisal from the Pharisees. His fear came mostly from the *inside*: the past sin still had a hold on him.

Suddenly Jesus appeared, passing right through the locked doors of their fear. Forgiving Simon, our Lord's first Easter words were these (John 20:21): "Peace be with you!" It was a sacramental handshake. Then Jesus put courage back into Simon Peter's heart: "As the Father has sent me, I send you." Beautiful, isn't it? The man just shown he couldn't be counted on, and our Lord turned around and made him the pope. Finally, Jesus said (John 20:19–23): "As I have forgiven and supported you, you must support and forgive others. You are to treat all people in the same way that I have treated you."

There is a sequel to Simon Peter's story. A few weeks afterward, Jesus met him on the shores of Galilee and asked, point blank, "Simon, son of John, do you love me?" It was a question demanding an unequivocal answer: "Do you? Yes or no?"

If it weren't for the Easter healing, I suppose Peter would have replied: "Well, I'm not sure. I let you down Good Friday, remember. I did deny you. I can't really be certain one way or another. I'm all mixed up!" But Peter never said those wishy-washy words. He said a straightforward *"Yes! You know I love you!"* He was able to say this, friend-to-friend, looking our Lord right in the eye, thanks to what Jesus did on Easter by instituting the sacrament of healing (see John 21:15–19).

That's what happens each time the sacrament is celebrated. Thanks to the power coming from Christ's death and resurrection, he can say the same to us. Using the voice of the priest, he tells us:

Notice how I'm treating you. I'm not bawling you out, not making you feel small, not rubbing your nose in the dirt, not even angry at you for taking so long to come to me. No, I am glad you're here so that I can tell you I forgive you and tell you to forgive yourself. See, I'm bringing out the best in you and celebrating the trust I have in your fundamental goodness.

Celebration runs all through the story. Jesus deals with us the same way he dealt with Simon Peter. He was not cupping his hand and whispering in Simon's ear, "Okay, I'll forget it this time, but don't do it again!" No. He was making a big fuss about the whole episode, displaying the delight and consequences of God's forgiving love.

That is what happens each time the sacrament is celebrated—delight and consequences. Yes, consequences. The sacrament is meant to be a "booster shot" as well as a celebration. Notice what Jesus said just before he left, on that Easter day. It was not an afterthought, but a part of the whole event: "As I have forgiven you, you forgive others." This was the *food* Christ meant when he told Simon to "feed my sheep. I have fed you with mercy and trust. Now you do the same for others."

We also have the sacrament of Easter peace from Jesus. His declaration of pardon is a gift, not a gesture. We have as much right as the first disciples to feel the healing of our failures. Thanks to Christ's graciousness, we are able to let go of all our bygone sins—all those acts of self-interest that came from our impatience or the desire for human respect.

Then, having been on the receiving end of love, we can put ourselves more genuinely into the giving end of it. When others reject us, deny us, slip into selfishness in hurtful ways, we need not act as pagans do—impatient, fault-finding, sulking, or getting even. No, not that. We have received—and *celebrated*—the power to act differently. We can forgive, care for others, and bring out the best in them the same way Jesus brought out the best in Simon Peter and in us. We can do this because Christ has already given us the "booster shot" of God's forgiving energy.

This is the way that healing happens. First we are loved by God. Then we take the trouble to experience it, to really let it sink in. Then we have the power and courage to love others in the same healing and patient way. And so we grow. God's love continues to be our enjoyment and employment.

And then one day, when we finally reach *our* version of the shore of Galilee, Jesus will say to us as he said to Simon Peter (John 21:16): "Do you love me?" We will remember especially the sacrament of forgiveness, and we will be able to say: "Yes, Lord! You know that I love you."

14.

The Fine Art
of Forgiving

Pulling Away from the Past

Let me begin with a true story from a sister who was a missionary in central Africa. The tribe she ministered to survived by trapping monkeys and then shipping them off to zoos all over the world. There was no trick to it. There wasn't even a trap—except the one the monkeys made for themselves. The method was simplicity itself. First, the villagers took a gourd, a vegetable something like a pumpkin, and emptied out the pulp. Then they cut a hole in the side of the gourd, just large enough for the monkey's hand and arm to squeeze through. They tied the gourds to trees, having placed a bunch of peanuts inside each "trap." Then they went home and waited for the monkeys to do all the work of making themselves miserable.

Yes, the monkeys were watching all the time. And they love peanuts! As soon as the villagers left, the monkeys climbed down the tree, reached in, grabbed a fistful of peanuts, and tried to climb back up. Nothing doing. The hole in the gourd was too small for them to get their fistful of peanuts out. If they squeezed their fingers together tightly, okay, but not if the hand made a fist. But to get "un-fisted," they would have to let go of the peanuts. No way! Those peanuts belonged to them!

So they were stuck, all night long, screaming with rage and fear. And the people just picked them up like milk bottles the next day. They were shipped off to live in some untidy zoo away from home forever—very unfree and very unhappy.

Pretty dumb, isn't it? One feels like yelling at the monkeys:

Come to your senses, monkeys! Let go of the peanuts! Your arm can get out the same way it got in, and you'll be free to swing on trees and eat bananas and have all kinds of fun. If you stay the way you are, you're trapped. You've made yourself a prisoner of those stupid peanuts! Let them go and you'll be free!

The monkeys would not listen. Peanuts—those stupid peanuts—were more important than their life.

Very often, people won't listen either. The "peanuts" that trap people are mostly hurts—hurts that the memory makes a fist out of and won't let go. They are called by different names: grudges, resentment over some past disgrace, righteous indignation at "what So-and-So did to me!" Or it could be self-condemnation and self-reproach; forgiveness of self is just as difficult as forgiveness of others. All these add up to hurts lodged in the active memory—and the memory won't let go of them.

It's a strange thing about these human "peanuts." When we are holding on tight, it doesn't really matter whether we are justified or not in feeling hurt. As a matter of fact, I'm only talking about the "justified" kind of hurt. There is no other kind anyway. I've never met anyone who didn't feel justified in the unforgiving attitude he had taken for being treated unfairly at one time or other.

So we are all in the same situation. We've been hurt and our memories give us good reason for feeling rotten. But that's not the point. The point is that we simply can't let this hurt continue to erode our energies. If somebody put us down or did us dirt, that's her fault. God will judge her and forgive her if she is sorry. But if we keep nursing the grudge and keep touching the wound and keep feeling sorry for the hurt that she inflicted, then we are still controlled by the past, and the one who hurt us still has us like a puppet on a string. We are still hanging on to the peanuts, unfree and unhappy, just like those screaming monkeys. And that's *our* fault! Why remain miserable just to make someone sorry for what she did? What a frightfully expensive way to prove a point—letting ourselves be trapped in misery because someone has betrayed us in the past!

I am often amazed—perhaps enchanted—by the selective focus of attention so many people have when they come for counseling. For such people, the present time is only dimly recognized. Current affairs and the people they are actually living with are vague, hardly noticed. Nothing in the here-and-now is noteworthy at all. Instead, a rankling wound receives 90 percent of the person's energy and I am fascinated by the specific and dramatic way this "something from the past" is dredged up.

It seems as if I am asked, not to be of help, but to be an audience. I feel led into the back of the person's brain, where I am given a chair to sit in. Ahead of me is a *giant* screen; behind me, a well-used movie camera. The movie house is dark, musty, and unhealthy. The host excitedly gets behind the camera. The lights dim, the camera whirrs, and I am shown—with amazingly accurate commentary—a detailed documentary: *All That Happened—The Way It Happened: Now You Can Understand Why I'm Justified in Being Hurt!*

I find myself feeling quite uncomfortable, a guest-prisoner of a movie about something that happened long ago. I see the energy—a kind of masochistic pleasure—flowing from the film's producer/director. I marvel at how well-rehearsed and expertly reenacted the scenario is. I feel all this is accomplishing no good. I prefer to lead the person outdoors into the present time, where real life and good friends, and sun and rain are. I'd like to destroy the camera and refocus energy from past to present. I can't. No one can. Only that person—each person, you and I—can let go of the peanuts of those psychocinemas that continue to replay the failures of the past.

At a workshop I attended, the speaker made this statement: "Suicides are always committed in order to inflict pain on those who are left." This includes little suicides as well: drug addiction, alcoholism, televisionitis, hypochondria, addiction to nagging or sulking. The motive is all the same:

- I feel hurt, so I'm going to let my life deteriorate. In this way, I will inflict the pain of remorse on those who did me in!
- I'll get sick, or have a nervous breakdown, and then they'll be sorry for the way they treated me.
- I'll stay in my room and they'll worry about what happened to me.

•I'll insinuate that my auto accident was really their fault—
for making me so upset.
•I'll flirt with somebody else, and then he'll be sorry!
•I'll just sit and watch TV all evening and not say anything
so they'll know how badly they've hurt me.

"And then they'll be sorry!" That's the broken record of the
self-victimized suicide. Nobody is worth that kind of ven-
geance. The peanuts are too expensive. They come at the cost
of enslavement to the past.

Jesus told us, over and over and with frightening insistence,
that we must forgive others and ourselves. We must, if we expect our Father in heaven to forgive us. In the Our Father, the
one phrase—"forgive us the wrong we have done, as we forgive those who wrong us" (Matthew 6:12; see also Luke
11:4)—gets highlighted. Jesus continues the prayer with a post-
script: "For if you forgive the faults of others, your heavenly
Father will forgive you yours" (Matthew 6:14). Indeed, in St.
Mark's Gospel, *all* prayer is summed up with that one phrase:
"When you stand to pray, forgive anyone against whom you
have a grievance so that your heavenly Father may in turn forgive you your faults" (Mark 11:25). (See Matthew 6:9–15, especially vv. 14–15; also Matthew 18:35 and Luke 11:2–4.)

Without doubt, this is rock-bottom Christianity. No excep-
tions, no ifs, ands, or buts. Unfortunately, though, people usually think of our Lord's demand as a *law* he laid down, and
then everybody starts looking for loopholes in the law. It ends
up with a statement like this:

Yes, Jesus, that's a good law about forgiveness; but if you
knew how So-and-So treated me, you would understand
why I'm excused from the law. You would understand

why I must continue as I am, feeling sorry for myself for being hurt and watching for my opportunity to get even!

One thing is wrong with a statements like this. Jesus is speaking about forgiveness, not as a lawgiver, but as a doctor. If a doctor told his patient, "Listen to me. *If* you want to live, you have to breathe. You have to eat and sleep and have a healthy body, too. These are the necessary conditions for life," the patient would be foolish to reply, "That's a nice idea, doctor; but I find breathing a burdensome chore. I have good reason to be excused from your advice." This would be ridiculous. The doctor is not laying down a law, but simply explaining what *must* be if there is to be life.

Forgiving is to the spiritual life what breathing is to the physical life. That is why Jesus made this his rock-bottom condition for being a disciple. That is why, according to Mark, all prayer is summed up with the necessity for forgiveness.

The only time God can reach us is the present time. That's all there is, really. The past is gone; the future hasn't come yet. But if memory keeps churning up the past and won't let go of the hurts, our breath is choked off and it is impossible for God or friends to reach us. It's like trying to talk to someone preoccupied with something else.

We see what is at stake here and why our Lord insisted so strongly that we must forgive, not only for the sake of those who hurt us, but also—and even more so—for our own sake. We must let go of those peanuts and get out of the trap of our own making—the trap of rancor and bitterness and self-reproach. We must let go of all those hurting memories—just let go—soften our fists and gently pull away from the past. Then we'll be free and happy and able to live in the present with all our friends—including God, who always was our friend, still is, and always will be.

15.

Mastering Moodiness 1

Watching Out for Pity-Parties

I am sometimes afflicted with a "must please" driver. One of my obstacles to grace is the assumption that "I have to please everybody, all the time, or else I'm no good!" That is a serious quirk in my makeup. It needs healing, all the time. Here is one of many stories I could tell about myself to illustrate my point: Some years ago, I gave a retreat for 50 sisters. Forty-five of them liked the way I conducted the retreat; five definitely didn't. They even told me what irked them: "You are too entertaining to have anything important to say!"

I should have been happy with 45 out of 50—ninety percent is a good average—but I wasn't. I more or less neglected the others and tried too hard to impress the five. Of course, they became all the more put off when I came on too strong. I only made things worse, and lost many opportunities to help the 45 others.

For weeks afterward, I sulked. "Nobody appreciates me. I'm no good. Why try any more?" I had a real "pity-party" all by myself! Why did I fill myself with such ill-tempered accusations? There was a flaw in the "interpretation machine" in my mind. I could not judge myself correctly. I was thinking, "I must have 100 percent success or I'm no good!" That's what happens when I let myself be driven by the "must please" driver.

I'm working at this problem (you'll be pleased to know). It's slow, but little by little I'm letting Jesus do the judging. I'm just trying to do what I can with those available to me now.

I included this personal revelation because many people are in the same boat. Many years of counseling have convinced me of this. A man has *one* enemy among his fellow workers; a woman cringes from the character assassination of *one* friend; a child is unwanted on *one* occasion—and the wrongdoing *world* is the cause for self-recrimination. The person wronged has a pity-party and comes to the conclusion, "I'm a failure!"

Along with the "must please" driver, there is another variation: the "be-perfect" driver, which delivers ultimatums such as: "Unless I'm perfect as a spouse (worker, athlete, writer, helper, friend), I'm not okay!" People afflicted with this driver have many ways of putting themselves down:

- •I'd do anything to get Uncle Jim to stop drinking. I can't do it. What's wrong with me?
- •What can I do to get my child interested in serious matters? I keep trying and failing!
- •I wanted so much to be a success in life. Yet here I am, 48 years old, and what have I really accomplished?

The problem with either the "must please" or "be perfect" driver is one of judgment; we cannot accurately assess our own worth. Our interpretation machine is out of whack.

The solution to this problem has been given to us. Jesus Christ has told us: "Do not judge. Do not judge. Do not judge." Jesus is judge and he has told us how he will go about it. Read Matthew 25:31–46 for a vivid description of the Last Judgment at the end of time and of the particular judgment for each of us.

What consideration will Jesus use to arrive at a fair trial? The evidence does not seem to include faith or obedience to the commandments. These things are assumed to be important, but they are not mentioned as being actually calculated at the time. It is *love versus insensitivity to others* that is the singular set of weights used to tip the balance between blessedness and condemnation.

With Jesus as judge—no one else—the Last Judgment will be a social affair. Jesus will allocate the blessed and the cursed into two separate groups (as a shepherd separates sheep from goats). He will ask some simple, practical, homespun questions that demand, on our part, a summary response of *yes* or *no:* "Did you love other people, caring for them when they needed you?"

Our lives—the *accumulated* pluses or minuses of our whole lives—will give the answer. Contingent upon the answer will fall the judgment from our Lord's lips:

Either "Come. You have my Father's blessing! Inherit the Kingdom prepared for you from the creation of the world" (Matthew 25:34). Or "Out of sight, you condemned, into that fire prepared for the devil and his angels!" (v. 41). Jesus then lists six criteria for the judgment he makes: Exhibits A, B, C, D, E, and F. Then the case rests.

Exhibits A through E seem to proceed along one line of deliberation. Exhibit F seems to be something else entirely. The first five that tip the scales in favor of everlasting happiness are all success stories. Hollywood would call them happy endings:

A. "I was hungry and you gave me food" (Matthew 25:35). You can see the contented face filling with good nourishment, perhaps the belly rounding, ever so little, and the back relaxing.

B. "I was thirsty and you gave me drink" (v. 35).

C. "I was a stranger and you welcomed me" (v. 35). You can see the way contentment is replacing shyness as some stranger, like Oliver Twist, is invited to "consider himself at home, consider himself part of the family."

D. "I was naked and you clothed me" (v. 36). Another success obvious to all. Scene one: shivering nakedness; scene two: warm, comfortable, attractive clothing. What a difference!

E. "I was ill and you comforted me" (v. 36). Again, there is an obvious change in the person helped. The words of encouragement, the fluffed-up pillow, the news from home, the chicken broth. There was loneliness and pain before you came; there is now comfort. You may not have brought about a miracle of healing, but you did bring happiness by your act of mercy. And you can see what you did.

F. "I was in prison and..." (v. 36). Now, following the same mode of success story, Jesus should have concluded, "You got me *out* of prison"; or "you obtained a governor's pardon for the convict."

Jesus did not say any of these things. He did not plead for success or even advocate a happy ending. He only said, "I consider thoughtfulness done for others is thoughtfulness done for me. And so when you visited 'me' in prison, you proved

that you cared about me, as well as the one who was prisoner.
I really appreciate that!"

Exhibit F contains what are perhaps the most consoling of
all the words that Jesus spoke. Of course, he is talking about
everyone when he says:

> I consider what you do for needy people as having been
> done for me, personally. So, when you see a person hurt-
> ing from:
> •lack of self-confidence (hunger)
> •lack of approval (thirst)
> •anxiety about acceptance (a stranger)
> •obvious imperfection (naked to fault-finding observers)
> •sickness in heart or mind or body
> and you alleviate the suffering, I consider such kindness
> as having been done for me. I will bless you with happi-
> ness that will never end.

Then our Lord continues (there's one more item on his list;
don't miss it):

> Whenever you notice a needy one in prison and you
> show that you care, you earn my blessing. There are
> many kinds of prisons. The ones that people make in
> their own minds are much more formidable than iron
> bars: the shell of self-pity, the despair of failure, the ded-
> ication to sadness or a grudge, the abdication of life's
> hope which is the essence of drug addiction, alcoholism,
> compulsive eating or wagering or any other way people
> have to entrench themselves inside the steel cage of their
> own construction.

You would do anything to get them out of prison: to

cheer them up, to heal their self-punishing hurts, to give them hope again, to get them to say yes to life once more. But you don't seem to be able to do the job. They stay in their sulks, or in their cups, or in whatever compulsion. And you are powerless to help. Don't think you have failed them, or me, just because you haven't been success-ful. You did visit "me" in prison, even though you didn't help "me" to get out. I love you for the care you had. It is your patient kindness that I look for, not your success.

These consoling words are the basis for the art of healing the hurt that comes from feeling powerless to help someone you want so much to help but can't, because he doesn't yet want to be helped or doesn't want *your* help. Don't give up on him. Keep caring and do not get discouraged. Perhaps the ad-dict or tantrum-thrower will hit bottom some day. Then he'll be ready to listen to plans for escape from prison. Meanwhile, remember (make a sign and tape it to your bathroom mirror):

I am not responsible for the success or failure of anyone. I am only responsible for having cared and tried, and for the fact that I still care and still visit the needy "other Christs" in prison.

The other side of the coin—where the scales of judgment tilt down—is weighted with the word *neglect*. Exhibits A to F are all the same. Jesus indentifies with the people suffering from needs of every kind. He reacts strongly to impatient "write-offs" or callous refusals to care:

I was hungry, thirsty, shy, naked, sick, caged—physically or psychologically—and you did not care. You gave up on me and washed your hands of me and did not care! Because of this, I have no choice: You have condemned yourself to the place where you will nurse your selfishness forever.

As for the others—those who, for the most part, cared about people (even though not always successful in their attempts)—they will be forever happy in the Kingdom where kindly love is understood, enjoyed, and celebrated.

The scene, perhaps, will be something like the coaches and players watching a videotape of Saturday's football game on the following Monday. The game is over and this is the time for evaluating the players' performances. The coach doesn't say much; he doesn't have to. The evidence is right there. Everyone watches, judging how well or badly the game was played.

In the Last Judgment, of course, the "game" is our life, all of it, play by play, incident by incident, event by event, kindness by kindness, or unkindness by unkindness. There won't be any hurry. We'll see it all and tally up.

Jesus will not have to say too much, no more than he said he would in Matthew's Gospel. All will be quite obvious then, as obvious as football players watching in slow motion what they tried to do or what they slipped up on. We will say either: "Yes, for the most part, I did care. I did respond to the challenges of love as these came my way. Here is where I belong: with you, Jesus." Or we'll say: "It's obvious I don't belong here. Send me down where hate and rage and bitter feuds are the name of the game."

The rest is mystery. No one knows exactly how we will experience the final judgment. But there is no doubt about the *fact* of it. We also have clues as to how it will happen and motives to prepare ourselves for this most important moment. Since we already know how the scales will be loaded, it would be foolish not to weigh them in our favor. No impossible tasks are required, but quite ordinary things: kindness, unselfish caring, sensitive alertness to the needs of others, healthy resistance to the temptations of disgruntlement or despair. If we keep trying to live up to such a possible and practical ideal, we will be able to think of our final judgment as an experience we can anticipate with joyful relish instead of dread. We will also noticeably improve the grade of happiness in the world where we're trying to work all this out.

16.

Mastering Moodiness 2

Up-Spin on the Downers

I still have a letter from a high school girl who, twenty or so years ago, expressed herself in a most beautiful way. When I gave a retreat at her high school, one of the assignments, or "homework," I gave was to answer ten questions that asked for honest responses to different aspects of life. They would write out their answers, leave them anonymous, and give them to me the next day. Sometimes I would read them out for everyone to hear and reflect on.

Here is one I read to the retreatants, her answer to these questions: "Everybody has a problem. What's your problem? How many ways can you think of to solve it?"

My problem is myself. I don't like myself. I'm always making a mess of something, somehow. Solution: I can start looking for my good qualities (if I can find any). I can remember that other people are having trouble, too. And I can always remember that God made me, and I have no right to throw it all back at him and say, "Can't you do better than that?"

The girl could not find one thing to say in her favor. Apparently, all the reports from family, school, and friends concentrated on the bad side of her conduct and character. She summed herself up as a dejected and rejectable "mess-maker"—a problem to herself.

In the cartoon strip "Peanuts," Linus is warning Charlie Brown's kid sister, Sally, "I think you should stop saying 'nyaah, nyaah, nyaah' to Charlie Brown. Those 'nyaahs' can hurt."

Sally retorts, "Oh, don't be ridiculous!"

"Well, they do hurt," Linus insists. "Those 'nyaahs' can get down in your stomach and really hurt."

"You're crazy!" Sally says. "A few 'nyaahs' can't hurt anybody!"

"They can," Linus concludes. "They can—if they become infected."

These two examples are present-day formulations of Job's bitter soliloquy about the terrible misfortunes that had so recently afflicted him. The once wealthy, now miserable poet bemoaned the dreariness of his life with words that speak for the clutch of sadness of every person, of every age (Job 7:1–4, 6–7):

Is not man's life on earth a drudgery?
Are not his days those of a hireling?

He is a slave who longs for the shade,
a hireling who waits for his wages.
So I have been assigned months of misery
and troubled nights have been told off for me.
If in bed I say, "When shall I arise?"
then the night drags on;
I am filled with restlessness until the dawn.

My days are swifter than a weaver's shuttle;
they come to an end without hope.
Remember that my life is like the wind;
I shall not see happiness again.

Although Job's tragedies were spectacularly sudden and pa-
thetic, the man's style of complaining sounds like it could
come from almost anyone. That's the way the devil usually
digs into us. Whatever it is that we love and cherish, he finds a
way of making it all seem cheap and humdrum and soon per-
ishing ("My days are swift, now . . . they come to an end without hope"). Very often, he has been our bedfellow as well
("The night drags on . . . I am filled with restlessness until the
dawn"). If being possessed means "letting the devil do our
speaking for us," we have been possessed many times, for we
have, many times, let the mood of gloom declare, "I shall not
see happiness again."

All three examples—Job's classic case of misery, Linus's
warning about put-downs, and the prayer of courage expressed
by the 16-year-old on retreat—all can serve as a model of how
everybody can be possessed at times by the devil of discouragement. All we have to do is stretch out the moments of Job's im-
pacted misery, the girl's messy self-portrait, and Charlie
Brown's "infected nyaahs," stretch them beyond imagination

to include eternity, and we have some idea of what hell will be. All we have to do is force the despair past any reach of hope; draw the gloom down over our eyes and heart; refuse to be consoled; resist anyone "pulling us out of it,"and we can sense the meaning of hell.

There is a saying, "All hell let loose." But hell doesn't "let loose"—it shrivels, selfishly uptight.

We've all seen people who have committed themselves to a living hell. A hurt, a loss, a cluster of "infected nyaahs" has really got them down, so down they don't want to get up. Their only occupation is to nurse their wounds: rub their grief until it becomes inflamed, justifying their hate-full grudge against the ones who hurt them, tricked them, jilted them, or simply left them hanging.

Try—just dare to try—to get them out of the bitterness that holds them fast. Try smiling or sharing something humorous you thought might cheer them up, and watch their scorn turn your smile into ice. Just try saying, "I know it's difficult, but I still love you. There is hope for tomorrow. You have gifts and talents and many friends. Don't throw them all away." Just try it, and you will be confronted with the same response Jesus faced when he came upon people possessed with an unclean spirit. They will brush your hand away, resenting and re-sisting the hope implied in your words of comfort, and re-spond with either sullen silence or bitter rage:

> Leave me alone. Let me be in my misery. Don't torment me with possibilities like hope or love or life renewed! I've dedicated myself to staying to myself—alone and un-consoled. The taunts of the people who hurt and tricked me and pointed out the mess I was making have so in-fected me that I can think only of the rancor and remorse in my heart.

Indignation is eating me up. Anger and self-pity burn in me like a fire that won't go out. I am nothing but this all-consuming thought of having been let down. So I will stay down. Neither God nor any friend can do a thing for me. Concepts like light and love and hope and life—these very ideas are the most repulsive things imaginable. Leave me alone. Let me eat of my bitterness. I am committed to despair!

You have met people who shrugged away your offers of consolation. It's very likely you have done some shrugging, too. I have. Thank God we didn't stay in our sulks too long. "Too long" is hell.

God does not condemn anyone to hell. The people who are there have, with deliberate and resolute decisiveness, committed themselves to be there. They have ignored God's warm invitation to be part of a Kingdom where words like care and love and kindness and life and gratitude are coinage. A world where such qualities exist is precisely what they find intolerable. The pride of wounded feelings is stronger than the hope of coming back to life again. Messengers of God's good news are greeted with an icy stare, justified resentments, and an unforgiving rage.

Such is hell: a place and a state of mind—fixed and inflexible—that prefers selfish brooding over hurts to happiness under any conditions. It is a cruel rendering of an old Ziegfeld song:

I'd rather be blue, thinking of you,
I'd rather be blue over you,
Than be happy with somebody else.

What can we do to keep away from that terrifying place? For one thing, we can let our friends and family exorcise us when we feel the way Job did. If an exorcist is someone who heals a person suffering from demonic possession, and if the common garden kind of possession is succumbing to discouragement, people can be exorcists in many simple, ordinary ways. All we have to do is let them cheer us up, help us face life again, make it possible for us to jump out of the sulk of depression.

People are available who can heal us with the healing power of Christ. And every time we let them, we are doing better than the possessed people of Galilee. We are not saying, "Leave me alone, Jesus of Nazareth. Have you come to destroy us?" (Luke 4:34) We are making it easy for our Lord to be of service.

I am not suggesting that we jump with joy all the time, which would be dishonest. I am suggesting that we let friendly care and new possibilities gently pull us out of the pit of self-pity. This is much better than letting "infected nyaahs" take over our whole system. Also (and most of all) I am suggesting that we let Jesus touch us with his light and love and programs for life renewed. The mean streak in our system is the devil's doing. Because he is sovereign over the kingdom of death and despair, we must escape his hold as quickly as possible.

Remember what the high school girl remembered. Even though hurts have infected our heart and we feel we shall not see happiness again, "We can always remember that God made us and (whether we feel like it or not) we have no right—we simply *do not have the right*—to throw it all back at God and say, 'Can't you do better than that?'"

17.

Looking at Heaven Differently

Jesus Replaces the Jokes

If someone could write down all the jokes about heaven, they would, I think, span the world a hundred times. Perhaps this is because humans don't like mystery (and nothing is more mysterious than life after death), so we populate the world of the unimaginable with anecdotes we feel at home with. Here are two stories of my own that illustrate the penchant to joke about heaven:

A few years ago, I was on the west coast of Ireland staying overnight on the grounds of a Passionist Monastery where there were some "traveling people" (once called tinkers) on a pilgrimage. Three of them were telling me that they definitely did not want to go to heaven. "Why not?" "Because," they replied in all seriousness, "Didn't Jesus say, 'In my Father's house are many mansions'? But who in heaven's name would want to be livin' in a mansion for forever!"

The next story took place in the 1960s. During a parish mission, I had the children all together for a couple of afternoons. I asked them, "Okay now, how many of you want to go to heaven?" They all raised their hands, except one boy in the back. The others, of course, pointed him out and said, "Father, Jimmy doesn't want to go!" Then I was stuck. "Okay, Jimmy, why don't you want to go to heaven?" He replied, with a hint of disgust in his voice, "Ah! You gotta be in church all day!"

These two stories exemplify how we replace awesome material with everyday trivia. We tame the sublime truths of our faith by reducing them to unremarkable experiences. And so, because of flaws in our own imagination, heaven becomes a boring, incommodious, sugary, pious *blah!*

Hold it! Erase these homespun conjectures. We have never been on the other side of eternity. The only human who has *also* lived in Paradise is our Lord Jesus Christ, and he has told us what heaven will be like. As a matter of fact, he spoke more about the necessity to strive for heaven than about anything else.

We would be discourteous (to say the least) if we refused to hear him out on this most important subject. Let's block off our tendency to think about God's mysterious world in terms of our preconceived notions or comical hunches based on our own lives.

Let us settle back, then, and listen to descriptions about eternal happiness from the only person who knows what he's talking about. Jesus hints about our eternal prospects in many different parables. His favorite stories about what heaven is like are that it is like the different ways we celebrate life: having a big party where everyone has a good time. See Chapter 15 of St. Luke's Gospel for an account of three such wonderful parties: when the sheep is found, the lost coin is discovered, and the prodigal son returns home. Joyful parties immediately get underway in each instance! The constant portrait painted by Jesus is one of immense enjoyment with everyone delighting in God's company, who pleads with everyone, "*Please* have a good time with all the others!"

And our Lord's favorite description is that heaven is like a wedding feast. It seems that in Galilee two thousand years ago (and to some extent, even today) a wedding feast "brings out the best in people." Grudges are forgotten, worries are left at the door, and there are no quarrelsome words and sad faces. The atmosphere breathes joy, appreciation of all present, friendship, and a kind of spirited dedication on the part of everyone to make this a day when they really live.

These are positive analogies—divine hints—about what our future world will be "somewhat similar to." Note that Jesus' emphasis is the attitudes we will enjoy, not the furniture around us. The next world will usher in a feeling of peace, absolute understanding, and a joy that no one will ever take away.

Still, the most telling aspect of Christ's revelation about the afterlife is his *negative* approach to the subject. The most comprehensive utterances are about what heaven is *not* like . . . what *won't* be there. We have to work things out from a few clues, but all the clues are there, in Chapter 16 of St. John's Gospel. The occasion was the Last Supper. As usual, our Lord was trying very hard to get his disciples to cheer up. They were disconsolate at the thought of his death. "The Lord is leaving us and we do not know where he is going." Jesus pleaded with them (John 14:1–3; John 15:11; John 16:22):

> Do not let your hearts be troubled. . . .I am indeed going to prepare a place for you. And then I shall come back to take you with me, that where I am you also may be. . . .All this I tell you that my joy may be yours and your joy may be complete . . . .I shall see you again; then your hearts will rejoice with a joy no one can take from you.

So all we have to do is itemize the thousand-thousand things that replace joy with worry, hurt, guilt, anger, or frustration, and these things will not be there.

I recently asked a class of first graders what took away their joy. Here is a partial list:

- Rain spoils my fun.
- My mother spanks me.
- I can't go camping.
- My pet gets loose.
- My brothers and sisters fight.
- I'm sick.
- I have to go to the doctor.
- The lights go out in a storm.
- My brother hits me.
- I have a stomachache from eating too much ice cream.
- I have no one to play with.

That's a respectable start. Now add a few thousand ways in which grownups feel their joy leaving them.

In heaven, not one of those hurts will be there. Not one! Everything that brings joy will be there, though, because God is the source of all that is good. Friends will be there, and family. But not the "not nice" side of their characters. We'll be there—but not our "bad side" either.

Exactly how will these things take shape? Jesus has not told us. How active will our memory be? What will we think of our past history? What will our thinking process be like? What will occupy us? How will we greet old friends, new friends?

Nobody seems to know. In fact, Jesus pointedly cut short all such conjectures. When the Sadducees tried to trip him up with the puzzle about the wife of seven husbands, he retorted (Matthew 22:29), "You are badly misled because you fail to understand the Scriptures." With the curt reply, he warned them not to conjure up fancies about life that is not within their range of experience (Matthew 22:23–33).

Actually, there is more here than just a quick rebuff. Jesus is giving us another important "negative clue" about heaven. He said, in so many words, "I cannot tell you about heaven because it is too much for you to comprehend right now. You'll have to get there first; then you will understand."

Our Lord was not putting us off or hedging. We ourselves do the same thing when youngsters ask us about things that are outside the range of their experiences. Even some first graders appreciated this fact. When I asked them if they could explain to their three-year-old kid brothers and sisters what it was like to be in first grade, they answered with an unarguable air of self-assurance, "Nah! They gotta grow up first!" These young children understood. Most of the life that they enjoy cannot be understood by younger ones. The tots will have to wait until they get there and experience it for themselves.

So it is with adults. Try to explain to a first grader some of the joys you experience: talking, for instance, for hours on end, with a friend who stimulates your mind and delights your heart, not knowing where time has gone (almost as if you had a taste of eternity). Try sharing this with a youngster and he will give you a "you must be weird" look and say, "What's so good about that? No fights? No toys? How could you have any fun just talking?" Then you would sigh and suggest, as Jesus suggested to his critics, that the youngster will have to wait until he grows up and develops a capacity for such an experience.

As a matter of fact, the contrast of before and after which Jesus makes is much more dramatic than adult to first grader or first grader to kid sister. At least there is *some* sharing of experience in my two comparisons. Tots, students, and adults are all human, with shared human feelings.

But Jesus goes all the way back for his reference point. "Compare the difference," he urges, "between the embryo in the mother's womb and a fully grown person with all his or her faculties intact. And compare the difference between a little mustard seed and the mature tree, big and branching, giving shade to the weary and shelter to the birds of the air."

Try to explain to a preborn in the womb what it's like to be a fully-developed human. Imagine yourself speaking to the baby inside: "Hey kid, I betcha you can't wait until you get out of there and grow up, right? Then you'll be able to swing on swings and feel sun in your face and eat ice cream and splash mud puddles and make friends and tell jokes and have all kinds of fun! I bet you can't wait until you can do all that kind of stuff, right?"

Wrong. The fetus could reply: "What is this weirdo talking about? What is sun? What are mud puddles? What are friends, and jokes? Impossible! Such things are absolutely unimaginable. Therefore, they don't exist!"

Then you would have no choice except to smile a thin smile

and shrug the shoulders a bit and say (as Jesus said to the Sadducees and as the first graders said to the three-year-olds): "Well, kid, you're just gonna have to wait till you grow up before you can understand."

Or to use another image, if an oak could talk to an acorn, it might say: "Hey, acorn, wait until you die and then are nourished by the sun and rain and soil. It's wonderful being an oak, swaying in the wind, enjoying the weather, letting children play on your limbs. It's really great, little acorn! I bet you can't wait to be a free-swinging oak like me!"

Doubtless, the acorn would not believe the whole idea. Or, if it were imaginative, it would wonder: "How could a closed-up, all encompassing seed possibly have limbs? How could it sway? And what is 'nourishment'? How could a 70-pound child climb on me? I'm no bigger than his thumb. Oak, you don't know what you're talking about!"

Compared to what we will be when we live heaven's lifestyle, we are as fettered and imprisoned as a fetus, or an acorn, or the tiniest of seeds. We simply have to take Christ's word for it that heaven is wonderful. Wait and see. You will know joy surpassing present understanding. You will experience life to be so free and stimulating that, compared to it, life in this world is miserable and drab. And the joy of your new life no one will take from you.

If we accept this on faith, what are the consequences—the practical "therefores"—in this present life? Granted that heaven will be a nice place to live, how do we get there? Do we simply "arrive" as a baby arrives, as a mustard seed turns into a tree?

And what about those "many mansions" in heaven? Are there "zoning laws" with the spiritually rich living in well appointed quarters, while those who "made it just at the last minute" reside in huts on the less pretentious side of town? Won't there be "haves" and "have-nots" there? Would that be fair?

When St. Therese of Lisieux puzzled, as a little girl, about such questions, her sister explained by asking her to fill a little thimble and a big pitcher with water. "Are they both filled?" "Yes." "So full they cannot hold another drop?" "Yes." "Well, that's what heaven will be like. Everybody there will be completely happy. They cannot possibly hold any more joy. But different people have different capacities for happiness."

St. Augustine expressed the same truth with a different comparison: "Heaven is like a beautiful, richly illuminated book. A child will enjoy it fully, as much as he is able; the texture has a nice feel to it; the colorful drawings are lovely to look at. An adult will enjoy all that the child does—and more—because he understands the meaning of the words."

Heaven will be something like this. Each will enjoy life to the fullest, according to each person's ability to take it in. The preeminently Christian work, therefore, is to let God increase our capacity for happiness while still on earth.

The "pitcher-full saints" have more to be happy *with*. Like an adult who understands the meaning of words, they will enjoy eternities of pleasant conversation, grown-up to grown-up, with God and the large-hearted saints.

Isn't that a consoling thought? Whenever we are kind to someone, sacrificing our own selfish needs for the sake of serving others (as Jesus did on the cross), whenever we study the words of Christ, pondering his ways, praying for deeper insights, we are growing in God's wisdom. Then, at the end of our life, we will be surprised. Wide-eyed with delight, we will see heaven for ourselves and say, "Look, God, all this time you were teaching me to speak your language!" And our Father will reply in words like these:

Yes, I know.

You have welcomed my Son when he came to you.

You have listened to his words;

you have lived like him.

Come up now, close to me,

for your place is heaven now.

You have learned the *meaning* of happiness—now enjoy it.

18.

Justice With Gratitude

Not Getting Anything Out of It

The term "user friendly" is the coin of the realm, these days. Whether we talk about software or hardware, outerwear or underwear, it is all one. The focus of the pitch is on the potential buyer, client, user. Years ago, the McDonald's chain came up with a song that summed up this service-oriented mentality. "Hey!" it declared, "You're the one! We do it all for you-u-u!"

Such emphasis is commendable in many ways. After all, Jesus told us to be "user friendly," in a sense. He insisted, "I am with you, not as one who is served, but as one who serves." And he warned us, in no uncertain terms, that we must never "Lord it over others." We must be sensitive to the needs of all, and be of service to them.

But to carry that phrase so far that we demand that God, family, friends, everyone be "user friendly" toward us—this is wrong-headed and causes wrongdoing. We go against the Gospel (and against the principles of mental health as well) if we march under the banner of "user friendly" and expect everyone to measure up to the world of our making.

Considering all this, how would you react to an exchange during a Sunday morning brunch between Lucinda and Mario, sister and brother, 17 and 24 years old? They used to go to church at this hour, but now they are enjoying a pancake treat in their favorite restaurant, instead.

Mario: "What fools we used to be, right, Sis? To sit through a whole boring hour in church, with a bunch of hypocrites . . . and then leave feeling like 'What a waste that was!' Why should we go to church if we're not getting anything out of it? These pancakes are much more user friendly. Pass the maple syrup, will you?"

Lucinda: "Not only that. I mean, the fact that it's real boring, you know! But I have to think of my friends. They'd make fun of me and say mean things about me, if they found out I went to Mass every week. Christmas is okay—and maybe a wedding or something—but I've got to stay friendly with my friends. They tell me which user friendly things matter and which ones don't. You know?"

So often, Jesus is not taken seriously unless he can compete with user friendly services and whatever activities the in-group says are "in."

But Christ and his sacraments will never be relevant or adaptable to any quick demands. Did not our Lord die on a cross, outside the walls, condemned by people who were frustrated because he could not, or would not, agree to their wishes for a political, generous, and tax-free Messiah?

There are certain changes we'd like to see taking place in our world that God, it seems, doesn't pay much attention to. Certainly the sacraments have a more profound purpose than simply giving pleasure. Justice and gratitude are the virtues that function at Mass. Justice is owning up to what we owe someone. If we owe our neighbor ten dollars, we pay up. If we are the parents of a baby crying in the middle of the night, we get up and take care of the child, because duty is as much a part of justice as a debt is.

The "user friendly" formula does not apply in these cases. How can we say, "Why pay the money I owe my neighbor? I'm not getting anything out of it!" How could a parent say, "I refuse to go to all the trouble of changing that diaper. It's not doing anything for me"?

The concern of "What's in it for me" is not the point of justice. Obligation is the point. Whether we like it or not, we must be responsible to others and to the law. (And some laws are defined; some are unwritten laws of responsibility, like parents taking care of their child.)

Now, then, what about God? How do we own up to what we owe to the One who created us and nourishes us with sun and rain and gives us hope for the future? God already has everything; so there is nothing, really, we can give God. The only way we return something to God, for all that has been given us, is gratitude: acknowledging that we did not create ourselves or keep ourselves alive. We are incapable—all on our own—of enjoying the benefits that engage our interests or that help us thrive in the world we live in. Ultimately, this is the work of a kindly, caring God. It is right and just that we appreciate these facts and tell God, somehow, of our gratitude, which is the virtue that always thinks of the *other*; it does not concern itself with "What am I going to get out of it?"

Of course, were it not for Jesus (and the prophets who prepared the world for him) we could thank God any way we felt like it. We could worship snakes, or walk solitary on a secluded beach, or say words of thanks over the Sunday pancakes.

But when the gift of faith has united us with Christ, we don't have such options any more. Jesus has taken the initiative:

> If you want to please my Father, and thank him for all that you are and have and hope to be, this is the way that will please him best: together, as people of faith, at least every Sunday, show God how things are with you. And through me, with me, and in me, in the unity of the Holy Spirit, give thanks and glory to God, forever and ever. Amen.

That's the way to say thank you best. Justice joins with gratitude and together they give God perfect praise.

Consider these two stories. The first one is on me. When I was a little boy, I gave my mother a left-handed baseball glove for her birthday. She didn't play baseball; and she wasn't left-handed. I did and I was. My dad talked to me that afternoon. "This was a gift, right, son?" "Yep." "For your mother, right?" "Yep." "Well, don't you think she ought to have something to say about it?" "(Gulp . . .) Yep."

That is the first time I learned that gift-giving is more than just remembering the loved one; it is also thinking of what will please the other person and doing something that will say "thank you" in a way he or she can understand.

Another story. Suppose you are graduating from high school. How would you like it if your grandparents gave you a

gift of a record of Sammy Kaye or Bing Crosby or some sing-
ing group popular in the 1940s? You'd be very disappointed. If
they wanted to give you music, at least they could find out
what kind of music *you* like. The very nature of a gift is "What
will please the *other*?" It is not "What am I getting out of it?"

The very nature of a gift, a *true* gift, demands the shift of focus from me to you. Tradition supplies certain occasions
where the expected thing is to remember a loved one's birthday or say Merry Christmas to him or her. On these special
days, the gift is a sign of love and a treasured way of saying
"thank you" for the friendship or family bonds or marriage
vows.

The gift-giver spends some time, first of all, reflecting on
what will please the beloved. If she "drops a hint" about what
she would like for Christmas, he doesn't mind the trip to the
store, the traffic jams, the money he could have spent on himself. He's glad to do it. It is something that he knows, before-
hand, will make the "other," happy.

So it is with the Mass when considered as a sign of our gratitude to God. The Mass is not the *only* gift we can give; it is not
the *only* way to thank God. It is—and only faith can make this
statement—the "thank you" that pleases *God most.*

We give gifts to those we love because of the love between
us. So faith demands, in justice, that we thank God for the love
God has already had for us.

How has God loved us? Besides creating us and caring for
us, benefits that all religions understand, the Christian faith re-
veals that God loves us even more intimately, even more personally. God the Father sent his Son to be born of Mary, to
grow up as we do, to teach, work, heal, die on a cross, and rise
from the dead to give us hope. God's concern was not, "What
will I get out of it?" God had the same concern all mature peo-

ple have when they give birthday presents or Christmas gifts to those they love. Mature people ask, "What will please the other? What will be the best way to let them understand that I love them and am grateful for our friendship?"

Christ's intimate and personal proof of God's love for us is the basis of our responsibility to love God back. We are in debt, so to speak, to love. Somehow, it is right and just to show our appreciation.

Of course, if we do get something out of the Mass, fine. The church, hierarchy and laity, has been trying to make the Mass as meaningful as possible. But this is just a fringe benefit. Sometimes the Mass really moves us; sometimes it is boring, and we feel like a bump on a log, like we're wasting 50 minutes.

Even so, we're thanking God, honoring God, whether we get anything out of it or not. Our love is other-directed; our gift of gratitude is focused on the person loved, not on self. This gift of thanks, which keeps the communication lines open, signifies the hope that our life with God may continue to grow. It says, as the Second Eucharistic Prayer puts it: "We thank you, Father, for counting us worthy to stand in your presence and serve *you.*"

We are no longer immature donors of left-handed baseball gloves or records of music which are friendly on the wrong side of the exchange. We are responsible—and responding—creatures, whose faith teaches us how to own up to what we owe to our Creator and Savior. And we know by faith how glad God is to love those people who can love God back. On both sides, it is a magnificent interchange—consideration and gratitude at its best.

19.

Mary, Model of Prayer

A Personal Meditation

This book has looked at different ways by which we help Jesus help us. Now, at the end of the book, it is right to consider how Blessed Mary did it. She was the finest example of how to allow God's will to work in us. Please read the following meditation about our Lady's prayerfulness and "love style." Read it slowly and, if it feels right, make it your own prayer, too.

Blessed Mary, teach us how to pray. Give us your *let be* spirit. Guide us to the present moment of our lives and let us live it as you did.

Every good instinct tells us the saints and artists were right about you all along. You had no "hang-ups" about the past, no worries or hurt feelings dragging down your ability to *be*. There were no preconceived notions about God—except that God is wise and powerful, creative and caring, nourishing and gentle. You are there—simply there—one day in Galilee: calm, unruffled by your past, unworried about your future. Serenity was the word for you, serenity that allows for life. You were the "good soil" the prophet Zephaniah spoke of when he commanded the Chosen People, "Rejoice, O soil of mine; the Lord is with you."

Good soil you were, able to be planted by the grace of God's own doing. There you were, that day—simply there.

And then it happened. You didn't do anything. It was done to you. God took the initiative. It was *God's* plan and timing, *God's* devising. The Father had a brilliantly creative idea. He would live up to his promise of salvation by loving the world and leading all people to the fullness of life.

God would do this in an ingenious way, sending his own, his only Son, into the world. God would be made flesh. This God-made-flesh would begin as a baby, so that we need no longer fear him; he would grow up slowly, so that we could learn patience; he would teach in parables, so that we could understand by means of familiar experience; he would ratify what he taught by how he healed, so that we could know that God wants to make us whole in every way; and finally, to show that all this was, indeed, the work of God, he would display the greatest proof of love on the cross. Then the Father would display the greatest proof of power by raising to glorious life this Son of God become a mortal man.

God had this lovely plan in mind. But since it was a plan of love, he could not force anyone to take part in it. His plan could not start unless he could find a human to be the freely-agreed-to mother of this plan. He asked you and you agreed.

As simple as that. You didn't *do* anything. You let it *be done* to you.

We take it so much for granted, Mary. The whole plan was started so beautifully that we somehow take you for granted. But how terribly it would have worked out if you were like us in your responses. We are so often filled with the hurts of the past. Like monkeys, we "won't let go of the peanuts" of our remembered injustices or the failures we brooded over. If you had been like us, you wouldn't have even heard God ask you for this favor. You would have been busy sulking over old wounds. Or you would have said, "Why ask me, God? I'm too shy, or I'll only do it wrong for you. I don't have the talent or the time."

These are the things that get in the way of our being "good soil" for God. But none of this got in your way, Mary. You were free of the tendency to brood or sulk or get all tangled up in the past. You were *now*, living in the *now*, ready to receive what God had in mind.

And you were not anxious about the future, either. I might have said, if I was in your situation: "Why pick me, God? What's the catch? I've got to find out more about what you're asking, before I agree to anything! What kind of sacrifices does it demand of me? Will I have to travel, or can I stay home?"

It is inconceivable that you would have said such things. But I do and probably most humans do. We are so afraid of the future. The dread of losing what we have is the poison we inhale. We are preoccupied with "What will I say next? How will I get along? Who will my friends be? What will become of so-and-so?"—all kinds of *what ifs* about the future. We are going so fast that our tomorrows seem like they are here already, and the present time has gone before we lived it.

Please, Mary, help us to slow down. Help us to live without

the erratic tugs of anxiety, without the self-defeating drain of
pacing our life according to other people's expectations . . . or
our own. Help us to say, with you, "Let it be done to me as
you say, my Lord—even though I'm not sure yet what it all
means. I trust your wise and gentle care. With your grace in
my heart, I am in your Kingdom. Let it be done according to
your will."

That's the way it was with you, Mary of Nazareth. And it
was done. The Word of God became your flesh. And, in God's
time, you brought forth the Word of God, made of your flesh,
for all of us to share.

Surely, Jesus was unique. He had a power and personality
all his own, yet your influence was always there. He was the
only child of whom it could be said, literally, "He has his
mother's eyes." Your eyes, Mary, and so much else: your
warm and gentle ways, your spirit of prayer (Was it not you
who taught him to pray?), your love for the Scriptures, and the
many other ways that made you who you were. Country, culture, traditions, training, family background, and so much
else—all these influenced your Son.

And what about the little things that we have not been told
about? Did you and Joseph plant a mustard tree in your front
yard so that Jesus could watch it grow through the years? Was
it you who lost a coin and "searched diligently until you found
it and then rejoiced with all the family because you found what
had been lost"? Was it you who rocked your child to sleep with
the story about how the mother hen cuddled her young ones,
safe and warm, under her wings? How many other things did
you and Jesus share together that we can only guess at?

Whether at home in Nazareth, with kinsfolk at Bethlehem or
Jerusalem, among your friends at Cana, Jesus was a part of
you—his own person influenced by your personality.

Since Jesus sent us his Holy Spirit, we are all "Mothers of God" in a way. When we hear the Word of God in the Scriptures, and when we receive Jesus in Holy Communion, we are doing the same thing you did, Mary—on a smaller scale, but it is the same reality. We let the Word-made-flesh become our flesh. He takes our personality as he did yours. We have the same power to "bring him forth," made of our flesh, for others to share. We have our homes, our ways of being nourished, our culture and customs, training and traditions—our own versions of the trees we planted, the coins we've found, the lullabys our mothers crooned to us—the simple joys like yours.

We too can bring Jesus forth, influenced by all these things that make up our personality and natural talents. We can, *if* we develop the spirit of prayer that you enjoyed.

Help us, Mary. Give us the resolve to make prayer a top priority in our lives. We usually are so sporadic in this matter. When we *need* something, and don't know any other way of getting it, then we pray. Sometimes when we are enthralled by beauty, or when we are in a peaceful setting, then we can offer spontaneous prayers of gratitude. A spectacular view of natural beauty, the hushed times when insights come unbidden, the stimulating moments of personal triumphs—these peak experiences stimulate everyone's prayerfulness.

But prayer, if it is to be "good soil," must be more than this. Guide us, Mary, to your Galilee. Teach us every day to have your *now* of Nazareth. Give us a hand to get us out of our pits of depression and hurt feelings. Be the good mother hen, folding your serenity over our hassled nerves and anxious worries. Slow down our pace. Help us to resolve, at least a half hour of each day, to be like you: in a silent place, ready to receive God's Word.

Let us do this important work and take it seriously. People

have so many different ways of making themselves sensitive to grace. Some pray alone; some pray with others. Some say your rosary; some do Zen or breathing exercises. Some walk outdoors; some sit in church; some have a quiet room where a picture is displayed or a candle lit. Some use a sacred word, repeated over and over, to help them live in the present moment; some use a holy book to ease themselves away from the gloomy past or the fearsome future. Some write down their prayer (as I am doing here); some recall a scene of Scripture and put themselves into it, waiting for what God might possibly call out from this.

All these are good. It's a matter of temperament and training, for the most part. Even so, while we call it prayer, we really don't do the praying. We don't, any more than you did. We simply let it be done to us. For the Kingdom of God is within us. At God's initiative and timing, the spirit of Jesus in us prays to our Father. We simply get the soil ready. Our work is to be in the here-and-now, attentive to the possibilities of God's active grace.

It may be that we just "waste" this half hour of each day. Many days it will seem to be just this. But it will not be wasted. (Were those years you prayed before the Annunciation *wasted?*) It may very likely be that prayer will be more simple and peaceful as the years roll by . . . like any kind of intimacy. No matter. Even the development of our prayer style (and the changes in our kind of prayer) is God's work, too. All we need to be is faithful to it.

For this we need your gentle guidance, Mary. I need it. We all do. Fill us with the spirit of your serenity. Soothe our tensions so that we can let it be done to us, according to God's Word—the Word made of your flesh . . . and thanks to you, now made of our flesh, also. Amen.

Afterword

Patience . . . Patience . . . Patience

Most people are good. You, gentle reader, are a good person. (Bad people wouldn't even pick up a book like this.) But I say you're good; I did not say perfect. The flaws you have are my flaws, too. And practically everyone else's. They fall in line within the time zones Jesus alluded to when he kept insisting that we must control those three obstacles to growth:

1. Do not judge (past).
2. Do not get discouraged (present).
3. Do not worry (future).

Past: We hinder God's grace if we use up time and energy judging the past sins of others (or their faults or their eccentricities or their bothersome behavior). We also destroy God's possibilities if we refuse to repent of our own sins as well.

Present: We frustrate Christ's plans if we let depression or wrath become our overriding passion. Both sadness and anger are emotions and, as such, are not sins. After all, Jesus wept because the people of Jerusalem turned their backs on him; and he often vented his anger against hypocrisy. The feelings we have about what is wrong with our present situation are unhealthy only if we let these feelings control us, when nothing engages our attention except our *right* to be angry or to be depressed. If such attitudes have completely taken over our minds, how can we be attentive to God's will? It is as if Jesus is trying to reach us on the phone, but he can't be heard because the "jackhammers of anger" or the "soap operas of our miseries" have usurped the airwaves, preventing all communication.

Future: God's love can also be blocked when we let forebodings of the future rob us of our energies. All our worries about "What if this happens or that happens" mean that we are fretting over a time that has not come yet and ignoring the only time that is real—*now*.

These three obstacles prevent Jesus from helping us to be healed. We have already named some of the various forms of judgmentalism, discouragement, and anxiety in this book. We must do our best to make sure they do not do their worst to us.

Of all the ways to help Jesus help us in this lifelong task of removing these obstacles and grow, the most important is to resist the negative effects of perfectionism. God did not put us here so that we might become perfect machines, always win, and never make wrong decisions. Such an ideal will never happen; God does not expect it from us.

Of course, this anti-perfection campaign goes against much of our moral, educational, and athletic training. We were brought up to honor the adage: "If a thing is worth doing, it's worth doing perfectly!" Something like that. That statement, literally applied, has malignant consequences. From it, we tend to criticize severely whatever is imperfect. We become despondent because we live such a flawed and incompetent existence, and we fill up with worry because our world will probably *never* reach the level of our wishes!

Because much of the world's standards are against patience, we have to labor daily and undauntingly against the tendency that pulls us toward perfectionism. We must work on patience in every area of our lives, and even be patient with our impatience.

These are not my ideas; they are the moral of many of Christ's parables. Of all of them, the feature parable in St. Matthew's 13:24–30 is the most dramatic and dynamic.

"The God-Movement of Grace (or the Kingdom of God) is like a man who sowed good seed in his field." It was all good seed, as Jesus readily admits. The design on the part of God and the farmhands was that there be a perfectly good field of rich grain.

The parable continues: "But while everybody was asleep, his enemy came and sowed weeds among the wheat and went away. When the crop began to mature and yield grain, the weeds came up as well."

The curtain falls on scene one. If we take the symbols away, the story is familiar enough. It is the very stuff of history, of scuttlebutt at work, of neighborhood exchange, of conversation brought up at home, of the seven o'clock news, of all of us—globally and individually—all over.

Weeds and wheat is the story of good and bad in us and others and in nations and neighborhoods. Good and bad exist together, growing out of the same soil, taking energy from the same sun, watered by the same rain, swaying in the same wind, holding on to their roots with the same tenacity. In self, family, church, world—in all of us—there is the "mixed field" of caring and selfishness, resolution and despair, acceptance and jealousy, spontaneity and sullenness, cooperative love and callous manipulation, the celebrations of life and the ceremonies of death—the good and the bad "growing up together."

Scene two: The servants in the story notice what is happening to the wheat field. (They are as perceptive to what's wrong as gossips are; they are as sensitive to imperfection as we are in our most disgruntled moods.) They see the weeds, and *they don't like them!*

(These farmhands represent us, remember—us "good people" who belong to Christ and who really care about the Kingdom.) They see the weeds and their impulsive response is twofold: impatience with the imperfection of the field and an impertinent blast of anger against the master who let it happen: "Lord, didn't you sow good seed in your field?"

"Yes, I did," the master replies.

At that, one can almost see eyes fill with fire, muscles tighten for a fight, disappointment in the heart forgetting to know its place, letting mouth erupt with the demand, "Then tell us, *Why there are weeds?*" ("What's the matter with you, God? If your intention is to have a good crop of wheat, what's the reason for all these imperfections existing side-by-side with the good?")

"An enemy has done this," is the simple reply.

Then comes the further impatient gesture. Compelled by the energy of indignation, the farmhands ask permission to destroy the field: "Give us leave, Lord, to root out all the weeds!" It is as if they said, "Trample on the imperfections! Put sickle or sword to them! Sins and selfishness have cropped up in myself, in my family, in my community—these are unbearable! I cherished so dearly that I would have been perfect by now. I had hoped so strongly that my children would become what I wanted them to be. I had so reasonably expected that the church would be made up only of saints, that fellow workers would all be fair, the people would all live up to their promises, and that love would sway the world."

But that is not the way it is!

And the reaction to this fact? "I don't like it! And I'm going to do something about it; nag the family even if it means rooting out their joy or hope in life; retaliate with violence against the spotty, vaguely functioning, imperfect plans of church, world, or neighborhood. I'm going to vent my anger and put teeth into my righteous indignation. Give me permission, Lord, to cut down all the weeds, and judge the world (or me, or both) as bad!"

In scene three the master appears again. He could be almost forgotten in the vehemence with which the servants concentrated on what was wrong in the wheat field. The servants probably didn't even expect an answer from the master. If he did answer, it was assumed that he would simply rubber-stamp the decision for uprooting, which they had already decided on. Something like: "You're right, boys. The wheat fields of my world have most certainly gone to seed and have yielded weeds. I guess there's nothing we can do but put the demolition squad to work and give those weeds a lesson they'll never forget, even if it means destroying the whole field in the process."

That's the kind of comment the servants expected. It's also the kind of response most supposedly "good" people expect from God when they are bitter about the imperfections in themselves and others. That's what makes the master's reply so striking, so surprising. "And the master said, 'No!'" He

doesn't rubber-stamp the servants' wishes at all. He doesn't
even suggest they calm down a little before they go out with
their weedkillers. He doesn't mollify them with a wishy-
washy comment such as, "Well, okay, if you feel you *have to*;
but try not to pull the wheat up—be *careful*."

He says none of these things. He says it straight: "*No!* You
have no permission to indulge yourselves with any methods of
destruction on the wheat fields of my world. *No,* and that's final!"

Then, after the negative, comes the positive commandment:
"*Let both* wheat and weeds *grow together* until the harvest. Then
I will judge the good and the bad; *I* will weed out those who
have given themselves up to imperfections. Your job is not to
weed out, or judge, or destroy. Your job is to make sure things
grow. Besides, you can't really tell, from your vantage point,
what are weeds and what are wheat. Look at your own past.
Wasn't it that miserable year (maybe in high school or whenever that time in your life was when you felt adrift and root-
less) that now, in retrospect, turned out to be so valuable?
Didn't you have to go through the darkness—frightened and
lonely—in order to come to understanding? Yet your parents,
your friends, even yourself perhaps were classifying that dis-
mal time as 'weeds':

'What are we going to do with our restless son?'
'Why is our daughter so unhappy?'
'When am I going to find myself?'
'What's it all about?'

"Now you see the time as the 'growth of the wheat.' It was a
period of life you are glad you had, for it was then that you developed self-assurance through trial; it was then that you

formed a capacity for compassion; it was the time, most of all, that made you aware of my grace 'raising you up' from your own self-stunting depression."

The better we clear out of the way all the negatives that block Christ, the better we will be in every way. When Jesus says *no* as he does in the parable, he is really teaching us how to say *yes* to life. We are called to help Jesus as he continues to knock on our doors, ring us up, call for our attention. The more we make it easy for him to help and heal us, the better we will equip ourselves for the day when we are formally invited into the divine lifestyle of heaven. Then we will, at last, experience those joys for which Jesus worked so hard, lived so well, died so nobly, and rose again with such great power. The last words he said to his disciples are the Inaugural Address for all eternity and the perfect promise of our perfect happiness (John 16:20–22):

Do not let your hearts be saddened.
Do not be afraid.
A woman about to give birth
is sorrowful
because her hour has come.
But when she has brought forth her child,
joy makes her forget her anguish
because life has come into the world.

So, you are now in sorrow,
but I will see you again,
and your hearts will rejoice,
and your joy
no one
will take away from you.

Also by Fr. Isaias Powers

Quiet Places with Jesus
These 40 meditations begin with Scripture quotations, followed by reflection and step-by-step methods to meditation.
0-89622-086-9, 128 pp, $5.95
Audiobook: Three 60-minute cassettes, print material, $24.95

Quiet Places with Mary
24 guided imagery meditations are directed to living life in the image of God, as revealed by Jesus, with Mary as a companion.
0-89622-297-7, 160 pp, $5.95
Audiobook: Three 60-minute cassettes, print material, $24.95

Letters from an Understanding Friend
A creative way to reflect and meditate on the message of the Gospel, with inspiring letters from Jesus.
0-89622-413-9, 96 pp, $5.95
Audiobook: Three 60-minute cassettes, print materials, $24.95

Women of the Gospel
Sharing God's Compassion
Each of the 28 women in this book is sent by God to bring God's compassion to those in need on earth.
0-89622-521-6, 168 pp, $5.95

Fr. Ike's Stories for Children
This delightfully illustrated book contains 12 animal stories, each with a moral. Children are entertained, then led to see the Christian values that are the core of the message.
0-89622-370-1, 64 pp, $4.95

Available at religious bookstores or from:

XXIII TWENTY-THIRD PUBLICATIONS
P.O. Box 180 • Mystic, CT 06355

To order or request a free catalog of other quality books and video call:
1-800-321-0411